PARADISE LOST

NOTES

COLES EDITORIAL BOARD

Bound to stay open

Publisher's Note

Otabind (Ota-bind). This book has been bound using the patented Otabind process. You can open this book at any page, gently run your finger down the spine, and the pages will lie flat.

ABOUT COLES NOTES

COLES NOTES have been an indispensible aid to students on five continents since 1948.

COLES NOTES are available for a wide range of individual literary works. Clear, concise explanations and insights are provided along with interesting interpretations and evaluations.

Proper use of COLES NOTES will allow the student to pay greater attention to lectures and spend less time taking notes. This will result in a broader understanding of the work being studied and will free the student for increased participation in discussions.

COLES NOTES are an invaluable aid for review and exam preparation as well as an invitation to explore different interpretive paths.

COLES NOTES are written by experts in their fields. It should be noted that any literary judgement expressed herein is just that – the judgement of one school of thought. Interpretations that diverge from, or totally disagree with any criticism may be equally valid.

COLES NOTES are designed to supplement the text and are not intended as a substitute for reading the text itself. Use of the NOTES will serve not only to clarify the work being studied, but should enhance the readers enjoyment of the topic.

ISBN 0-7740-3393-2

© COPYRIGHT 2003 AND PUBLISHED BY
COLES PUBLISHING COMPANY
TORONTO - CANADA
PRINTED IN CANADA

Manufactured by Webcom Limited
Cover finish: Webcom's Exclusive **DURACOAT**

TABLE OF CONTENTS

BIOGRAPHY OF JOHN MILTON

England's great epic poet, John Milton, was born in London, England, on December 9, 1608. His father, disinherited by his family for deserting the Roman Catholic faith for Presbyterianism, made a good living as a scrivener and money broker.

John's mother, Sarah Jeffrey, was the daughter of a merchant tailor. Five children were born to Sarah and John Milton. Two of these died, leaving John's elder sister, Anne, and younger brother, Christopher.

The elder Milton, who had a great respect for learning and who was also an accomplished musician, cared deeply about his son's education. John was given a private tutor to encourage his interest in literature and music. This tutor, Thomas Young, a Presbyterian minister stayed with John until he entered St. Paul's School at the age of seven. He was an eager and proficient student who, even at the age of ten, tried to imitate the Roman poets. Much of his early verse was, in fact, written in Latin.

Milton's best boyhood friends were the Latin poet, Alexander Gill, an instructor and son of the headmaster, and Charles Diodati, son of a distinguished physician. His Latin elegy, "Lament for Damon" was his expression of grief at this friend's death.

At the age of sixteen, Milton took up residence at Christ's College in Cambridge. Here, he soon displayed his proud rebellious spirit by quarreling with his tutor, William Chappell, and had to be transferred to another more compatible tutor. The young man's haughtiness and emphasis on virtue also made him unpopular with fellow students, and earned him the nickname "the lady of Christ's". But scholastically Milton soon showed his exceptional talent. He distinguished himself in Latin poetry by writing Ovidian elegies and he excelled in academic orations. His first outstanding poem in English was the lovely hymn, "On the Morning of Christ's Nativity", written shortly before his twenty-first birthday.

Milton received his B.A. at Cambridge in 1629 and his M.A. in 1632. Milton's literary work of this period includes lines on William Shakespeare (prefixed to the "Second Folio"), two humorous epitaphs in octosyllabic couplets (on the demise of the marchioness of Winchester), and probably the companion lyrics, "L'Allegro" and "Il Penseroso", for which the exact date of composition is not known.

Throughout his early youth and college years Milton, who was intensely religious, had planned to enter the ministry. However, on graduation from Cambridge, Milton relinquished this plan due to his increasing dislike of the Church's emphasis on ritualism, and of the conformist dictates of William Laud, Archbishop of Canterbury. Instead, Milton decided to be a poet and to glorify God through the written word. He now moved back to his father's house at Horton, Buckinghamshire, where he stayed for the next five years, devoting himself to the study of Western thought and culture, and to composing verse.

During these years he wrote "Comus" (1634), a masque composed for the inauguration of the Lord President of Wales, and his greatest early poem "Lycidas" (1637). In this monody he bewails the premature death of a friend and he uses the young man's virtues as a contrast to the corruption of the clergy of his day, whose ruin he prophesies. These works of Milton's repeatedly illustrate his moral ideals.

Shortly after his mother's death, Milton's father sent the young man abroad on a "Grand Tour" to complete his education. In Paris, Milton met the Dutch jurist and statesman, Hugo Grotius; in Florence, he mingled with members of the Accademia degli Svogliati, a cultural organization, and formed a lasting friendship with Carlo Roberto Dati. In Florence, Milton also met Galileo. He talks about this meeting in his famous pamphlet on censorship, "Areopagitica."

Milton's European tour lasted two years. Then, the growing religious and political ferment in England drew him home. In the struggle between Parliament and Puritans versus Church and King, Milton allied himself with the Presbyterians which made up the largest part of the Puritan party. From then on, Milton saw himself as the poet of "the second glorious reformation." But he, in fact, became more pamphleteer than poet for the Puritan cause. Although a set of manuscript notes made within a year of Milton's return to England suggest that he was even then interested in the fall of man as the subject for an epic poem, he was to write mainly prose for the next twenty years.

Back in London Milton set up a school starting with his two nephews, Edward and John Phillips, and began writing pamphlets on the abolition of episcopacy. Milton opposed the bishops and favored the Presbyterian system.

In 1642, at the age of thirty-four, Milton married seventeen-year-old Mary Powell, the daughter of a Royalist Oxfordshire squire who owed money to John's father. The young bride was obviously unhappy with her stern, rather demanding husband. After one month of marriage she asked to visit her family. She did not return to her husband until two years later, when she begged his forgiveness. Their obvious mental incompatibility inspired Milton to write pamphlets attacking the canon law making adultery the only grounds for divorce. In his first pamphlet he maintained that mental incompatibility contradicted the spiritual ideal of marriage.

His tract on divorce brought Milton much unpleasant notoriety, and he now found himself in opposition to the Presbyterians he had previously defended. Consequently, he became an independent in both church and state matters. In 1644, Milton wrote "Areopagitica", a prose oration defending freedom of the press. In the same year he published a treatise on humanistic education.

Mary returned to Milton in 1645, and gave birth to her first child, Anne, the following year, and to Mary in 1648. During this period, Milton wrote a history of Britain (published in 1670), six sonnets, and a series of psalm translations.

The Tensure of Kings and Magistrates (1649) which was published after the execution of King Charles 1, endorsed the people's right to dispose of a tyrant. He defended the action on the basis of the democratic notion that sovereignty is only granted by the people, and may be withdrawn when it is abused. Because of his views, Milton was appointed Latin secretary to Cromwell's Council of State (1649). He held this post until the Restoration in 1660. Consonant with his office, Milton published *Eikonoklastes*, an indictment of the personality and career of Charles 1.

The years of public service were also for Milton years of much personal misfortune. A newly born son, John, died in 1651, and a year later he lost his wife and the new baby in childbirth. Now the poet was left alone with three young children. At the same time his health was failing and, in 1652, Milton, whose sight had always been poor, became totally blind. There is no doubt that his secretarial duties hastened the development of what is believed to have been glaucoma. But he continued to write—by dictation—and to compose the monumental *Pro Populo Anglicano Defensio Secunda* (1654), paying tribute to the leaders of the revolution. His secretary was the famous poet, Andrew Marvell.

In 1656 Milton married Katherine Woodcock—who died a year later, also in childbirth, along with a daughter. For years now his growing daughters were brought up by the severe, blind man, who is reputed to have been a harsh father, with little capacity for warmth and affection, but who probably just could not cope with the demands of these young women and his blindness.

In 1663 Milton married again. This time, twenty-four-year-old Elizabeth Minshull. Unfortunately, his daughters did not get along well with her son and soon left their home.

In 1660 Charles II had been restored to the throne, and it is a wonder that Milton did not lose his head during the purges of the Restoration. Possibly his life was saved by the pleas of his former assistant, the poet Andrew Marvell.

Milton's pamphlets, however, were burned in public, and he had to go into hiding. He also lost some of his property and, of course, his salary. Because of his prudent attitude towards money, however, Milton was not actually impoverished.

When Milton settled with his third wife in Bunhill Fields, after moving from place to place for several years, he was fifty-five years old. There he returned to the full time pursuit of writing poetry. In 1665 he finished the great epic poem so long on his mind. It was published in 1667.

A sequel, *Paradise Regained*, appeared in 1671. This was a serene work which amplified the theme of *Paradise Lost*. *Samson Agonistes* appeared at the same time and probably owes some of its greatness to the similarity of the blind hero's life to Milton's own.

During his last years, Milton also produced minor poems, Latin letters, a Latin dictionary, and a theological manuscript. He also did some pamphleteering against Charles II. Milton's idea at this time was to advance tolerance among religious sects. He believed that they should jointly regenerate sinful humanity.

Milton died of gout in 1674. He was buried beside his father at St. Giles, Cripplegate.

RELIGIOUS BACKGROUND

Throughout *Paradise Lost* Milton repeatedly states the main religious tenets underlying the poem: The fundamental sin of both the fallen angels and man was pride. (*Pride* is here used in the theological sense of putting one's trust in oneself rather than in God, and all other sins stem from it; this older use of *pride* should not be confused with its modern usage as a synonym for normal self-esteem.) Both Adam and Eve manifested this sin of pride when they disobeyed God's command not to taste the fruit of the Tree of Knowledge. Again and again Milton stresses that obedience to God's commands is basic to all virtue.

Milton believed that men have free will; free will has to be governed by reason. Eve allowed flattery to overcome her weaker, feminine reasoning powers; Adam allowed passion (his love of Eve) to overcome his stronger, masculine reasoning powers. Both sinned and had to repent and to accept God's punishment as just before they could hope for forgiveness and redemption. Having repented and acknowledged God's justice, they could be forgiven, but they still had to pay the penalty for their acts—in their case, expulsion from the Garden of Eden and, after suffering, Death. By the great paradox of Christianity, however, Death for true believers is the beginning of Eternal Life.

Much has been written about whether or not Milton was a Puritan. How orthodox he was in his religious beliefs is another question often raised. The answers, of course, depend upon the definitions of terms.

In the larger sense of the word Milton may be called Puritan; that is, he believed that man should seek the closest possible relationship with his Maker, unhampered by rites and formal prayer. On the other hand, most Puritans of the seventeenth century were Calvinists, and so believed in predestination. Milton certainly was not a Calvinist; no man ever was firmer is his belief in free will and the power of reason. (Consideration of Milton's obvious love of learning and music is beside the point here. Contrary to popular notions, many educated Puritans made no objection to anything cultural or aesthetic as long as, by it, man was led toward God rather than away from the Creator.)

Most of Milton's basic teaching in *Paradise Lost* is completely orthodox Christian doctrine. The possible exception is his presentation of the Trinity, a very complex point, and one in which terms have to be defined clearly, the changing definitions of words considered, and the necessity of presenting ideas graphically remembered. The reader of *Paradise Lost* should always keep in mind that Milton did not expect his descriptions of happenings in Heaven and his reports on conversations between God and His Son to be taken as literal truth, any more than he wanted the building of Pandaemonium in Hell to be regarded as other than symbolic. He carefully explains (see especially Book V, 563-577) that all has to be reduced to terms understandable to man, that spiritual facts can be represented only in material terms.

PARADISE LOST AS EPIC POETRY

1.   In classic epics the reader is introduced to the action at a particularly dramatic or interesting point; later, usually well before the tale is half-told, the earlier events are supplied. (If you consider the alphabet as standing for the action of an epic, the epic may be said to start at *e*; somewhere near *j*, the reader learns the events of *a*, *b*, *c*, *d*; then the chronological account picks up again at *k* to continue regularly for the rest of the poem.) This standard epic pattern is easily observable in *Paradise Lost*.

2.   The use of invocations (appeals to a power greater than the poet to help him in his task): In *Paradise Lost* books I, III, and VII begin with such invocations.

3.   The use of prophecy to foretell future events of great importance: In *Paradise Lost* Michael makes such a prophecy, a resume of Biblical history from Adam to the coming of Christ and the Redemption of man (Books XI-XII).

4.   The variation of the scene of the action from the home of the gods (Heaven) to Earth: in *Paradise Lost*, the setting is Hell, Heaven and Earth (especially the Garden of Eden).

5.   The use of a celestial visitant to warn mortals of some impending catastrophe or great event: In *Paradise Lost*, the Creator sends Raphael (Books V-VII) to warn Adam and Eve not to be betrayed into disobedience by the wiles of Satan; and He sends Michael (Books XI-XII) to tell Adam the all important news that man will have a Redeemer.

6. The inclusion of allegorical episodes: In *Paradise Lost*, the allegory of Sin and Death is told in two parts (Books II and X).

7. The use of dreams as forewarnings: In *Paradise Lost*, Eve's dream (Book IV) is an omen of the coming Fall.

8. Description of wars, battles, armaments, etc.: In *Paradise Lost*, Book VI is devoted to the War in Heaven between the loyal and the rebellious angels.

CHAPTER SUMMARIES
AND
COMMENTARY

BOOK I The first five lines of the poem tell with remarkable brevity the theme of the whole epic: Milton asks the Heavenly Muse to help him sing of man's first disobedience in tasting the fruit of the forbidden Tree of Knowledge, an act that brought Death and suffering into the world, with loss of Eden, until Christ restored man to Paradise.

The invocation to the Heavenly Muse continues (through line 26) and ends with the poet's great purpose, to "justify the ways of God to men." In other words, he wants to show that God was just in his punishment of man.

The second verse paragraph (lines 27 ff.) repeats the theme in more detail, then quickly reviews Satan's sins that caused him to be cast out of Heaven and into Hell: Through pride, he wanted to equal God and so had raised "impious War" in Heaven. Then the narrative proper begins with Satan and his followers suffering in a fiery Hell, but with the chief Fiend's pride unconquered.

On discovering Beelzebub "welt'ring by his side/ One next himself in power, and next in crime," Satan conceals the despair he is feeling and quickly boasts (lines 85-124) that he is unconquered, filled with hatred, and ready to find out how to revenge himself upon God.

Beelzebub flatters Satan in his answer (as he always does), but questions whether any rebellion on their part may not be part of God's plan (lines 128-155). Satan refuses to be weak. If God brings good out of their evil, they in turn will again bring evil out of that good. Then, seeing a "dreary Plain," he suggests that they find refuge there from the "fiery waves" tossing them (lines 156-191).

Having reached this place of comparative ease, Satan again asserts himself as the leader. The other fallen angels must also leave their first place of torture to join him and Beelzebub on the plain. He proceeds to gather his cohorts around him by a mixture of flattery (they have been the "Flow'r of Heav'n"), threats (of what may happen to them if they linger), and sarcasm (at their odd choice of a place to slumber or to worship their Conqueror, whichever they may be doing).

Milton then enumerates these fallen angels, now devils, by giving them the names under which they later were worshipped as false gods in heathen countries; each is very briefly characterized. Of the list, the first and last appear later in the poem: Moloch (lines 392 ff.), an Ammonite god to whom children were sacrificed; and Belial (lines 490 ff.), who was not worshipped in one place, but who filled with lust and violence many places of worship as well as courts and palaces, for he loved vice for its own sake.

To this gathering of devils, Satan makes a stirring appeal, but first excuses his late defeat. Who could have known the strength of the "Monarch in Heaven?" But the rebellious angels had been overcome by force alone, and so should carry on the war, if not openly then by "fraud or guile" (lines 622-662).

The fallen angels cheer their leader (lines 663-669). Then Mammon (from the Syrian word for riches), whose greed had been apparent even in Heaven where he kept his eyes upon the golden pavements, leads some of his fellow denizens of Hell as they ransack the hills for gold and other precious metals (lines 670 ff.). With amazing speed they build a palace, called Pandaemonium, for Satan and their other leaders.

At the book's end, all the devils flock to Pandaemonium, the lesser fiends becoming much reduced in size so that all can fit into the palace. But the leaders keep the great size that they had had in Heaven and meet separately in a "great consult" as to their future actions (lines 789-798).

COMMENTARY

CHARACTERS   Satan, Beelzebub, Moloch, Belial, Mammon; also a host of lesser fallen angels.

SETTING   Different parts of Hell.

THE PROLOGUE   (lines 1-26) This opening passage has been one of the most admired and most written about parts of the whole epic. Not only does it give a synopsis of the poem, but it also suggests the combination of Biblical and classical lore that Milton uses throughout the poem. He asks the "Heav'nly Muse" that inspired Moses to teach his people to help him as he wishes to "soar" above the Aonian Mount (Mt. Helicon), the home of the Muses. He would have himself made worthy of his great enterprise in justifying "the ways of God to men."

The writer's spirit of dedication is apparent. Both Milton and his reader realize the sacredness and the immensity of the proposed task. Above all, the prologue convinces its readers that no ordinary work will follow.

SATAN   In Book I, Satan (from the Hebrew word for *adversary*) appears to be admirable in his strength and steadfast purpose. He seems to be the suffering underdog, with whom we always have sympathy. Note, too, that Milton has given him many of the more moving (and quotable) lines in the book; for example, some of the lines with which he encourages his followers: "Awake, arise, or be for ever fall'n" (line 330) and "who overcomes/ By force, hath overcome but half his foe" (lines 648-649). (Such passages are particularly effective if taken out of context.)

In fact, Satan is so favorably drawn in Book I that he has been mistaken for the hero of the poem. More logically, some critics have wondered whether Milton had not made him the hero unintentionally, for no religious-minded man could rationally have the Devil as the hero of a poem dedicated to showing God's justice. Several points of logic and of dramatic skill have to be considered here in regarding the way Milton first presents the Devil. First, Satan has very lately fallen from his position in Heaven, near the Creator. Therefore he has not fully degenerated into the evil force that he becomes as the narrative continues. Secondly, the implied struggle for the soul of man that underlies the poem would be much reduced in emotional appeal if the Son of God did not have a worthy opponent in Satan.

Despite the generally favorable impression that Satan makes in this first book, careful reading of the text discloses the fact that Satan has started already on his path of deception, perhaps deception of himself as well as of his followers. For example, he sees God only in terms of his own cruelty and as a tyrant uncontrolled by any laws of justice; Satan also exaggerates about the number of angels that have rebelled against their Creator and joined his own cause, claiming as his followers one half of Heaven's angels, rather than the true one third. As Milton said succinctly, Satan's speeches had "semblance of worth, not substance" (line 529).

BEELZEBUB   The Devil has many names, and usually Beelzebub, "the god of Flies," is simply one of Satan's names. Milton, however, makes another character out of Beelzebub, and then shows him as Satan's sycophant and flatterer, the useful tool of any politician. This characteristic is especially apparent in Book II when Beelzebub adroitly manages the Council of Devils so that Satan goes on his mission to corrupt man.

MILTON'S HELL   For the purpose of his poem Milton had to have a physical Hell, and he provides us with an extensive one of brimstone lakes, dreary (and hot) plains, and volcanic mountains, all without light, in "darkness visible"; and finally, ornate, comfortable, well-lit Pandaemonium with "many a row/ Of Starry Lamps and blazing Cressets" (line 728). But even this physical Hell or more accurately, these Hells, for Pandaemonium is very different from the brimstone lake, are subjective, if Satan is to be believed:

> The mind is its own place, and in itself
> Can make a Heav'n of Hell, a Hell of Heav'n.

(lines 254-255)

More interesting to many modern readers than any physical Hell is that other Hell within Satan's mind, the Hell that we recognize as also within man's mind: "the thought/ Both of lost happiness and lasting pain" (lines 54-55); or, echoing Dante, Hell is wherever "hope never comes/ That comes to all" (lines 66-67).

THE LISTING OF THE FALLEN ANGELS (lines 376-521) Milton is not just showing his extensive reading in old mythology and folklore. Catalogues (or lists or enumerations) are characteristic of classical epics. In the *Iliad* (Book 11, line 484 ff.) there is a famous one of ships and their commanders.

PANDAEMONIUM (lines 756 ff.) The name means "all spirits" or "all deities." It is one of Milton's few coinages.

SIMILES AND EPIC SIMILES Book 1 is especially rich in series of comparisons that often include epic (or Homeric) similies. (In such similes the original subject being described often is overshadowed by the comparisons made; in the true epic simile the comparison comes before whatever is being described. For a perfect Homeric simile, see lines 768-776.)

In the description of Satan (lines 192-210), Milton conveys the fallen angel's great size by comparing him to the Titans of mythology and then to the Leviathan of Psalm civ.26; the hugeness of the Leviathan is elaborated upon at some length before Milton returns to Satan. Later (lines 283 ff.) the Fiend's size is again emphasized by comparing his shield to the Moon, and his spear to the tallest Norwegian pine that normally would be used for the mast of some great admiral's ship.

Even more famous is the series of similes (lines 301 ff.) that Milton uses to suggest how numerous the fallen angels are. The first (and most often quoted) comparison is taken from nature:

> Thick as Autumnal Leaves that strew the Brooks
> In *Vallombrosa* . . .

(lines 302-303)

The second comparison is taken from the Old Testament: the fallen angels are like the carcasses and broken chariot wheels of Pharaoh's army floating confusedly in the Red Sea during the pursuit of the Israelites. Some lines later the fallen angels are compared to "a pitchy cloud/ Of *Locusts*" (lines 340-341), then to the barbarians descending on Rome "like a Deluge on the South" (line 354), and at the end of the book to bees swarming:

14

>   As Bees
> In spring time . . .
> Pour forth their populous youth about the Hive
> In clusters . . .
>   So thick the aery crowd
> Swarm'd and were strait'n'd [pressed together] . . .

(lines 768-776)

BOOK II Book II is largely dramatic and narrative, in some contrast to the preceding book with its emphasis on description. The action begins with the leaders of the fallen angels gathered together in Pandaemonium in a "great consult" to decide what they should do next.

What follows has all the elements of a play satirizing so-called democratic leadership. As we learn later, Satan knows how he is going to attack God, but he allows a number of his more important assistants in the recent war in Heaven to give their points of view. (In this way Milton shows the weaknesses of different types of political leaders.) The participants in the debate have been introduced already in Book 1, but now the oration delivered by each shows his character, and in each a particular type of individual can be recognized. The first to make himself heard is Moloch (lines 43-108), the professional soldier. Interested primarily in fighting, he immediately advocates all-out war against God, regardless of the final outcome. On the other hand, Belial (lines 109-227) appeals to Satan's legions suggesting appeasement—peace and ease at any cost. Why go down in almost certain defeat? Why not enjoy themselves as much as they can under present conditions, and things may get better? Mammon (lines 228-282), the materialist, goes along with Belial, but puts his emphasis on the possibility of developing Hell and so improving their condition.

The hordes of fallen angels find Mammon's suggestion most to their liking. Therefore Beelzebub (lines 299-380, 390-416) swings into action. He is the politician in the lowest sense of the word, the mere mouthpiece of the person in power. Now he persuades the devils before him that, if rumor is correct, God can be attacked through his new creation, man. It remains for Satan (lines 427 ff.), not only the clever manipulator but also the leader who knows how to exploit his own bravery, to volunteer for the mission.

When Satan sets out on his journey through Chaos toward the Earth, the other fallen angels amuse themselves according to their desires and abilities (lines 521-628). Some play military games, some sing, some consider philosophical questions but are lost in "wand'ring mazes," some explore the place they are doomed to. (This listing of the ways in which the Devils spent their time is in the epic tradition; similar interludes are to be found in classical epics.)

In the meantime, Satan approaches the Gates of Hell (lines 643-648). These are guarded by two figures: Sin, begotten by Satan when he first became jealous of the exaltation of the Son of God, and her son Death. Sin is not only the daughter of Satan but his paramour; Death is the result of this incestuous union, as Satan learns. And Death, once born, promptly raped his mother.

Sin holds the key that locks Hell, but she is persuaded by Satan to allow him to pass through the heavy gates (lines 815-889). As a final touch in the allegory, Sin cannot close the gates, which remain open forever.

In the last section of the book, Satan travels through Chaos (lines 889 ff.), meeting briefly Anarch, its ruler, who gladly sends him on is way to wreak destruction (lines 951-1010). The book ends with Satan catching sight of his goal, Earth (lines 1034 ff.).

COMMENTARY

CHARACTERS Satan, Beelzebub, Moloch, Belial, Mammon; Sin and Death; Anarch (Chaos).

SETTING Pandaemonium in Hell; other parts of Hell; the Gates of Hell; Chaos.

THE "CONSULT" OR COUNCIL IN HELL (lines 1-505) Milton had many possible sources for his famous council scene in Pandaemonium. First of all, as Latin secretary under Cromwell, he had been present at councils of the Commonwealth leaders. But such scenes are to be found in other epics, notably the *Iliad* and *Aeneid*. (One critic—Marjorie Nicolson, *John Milton*, pp. 196-197, 204-205—sees Pandaemonium as St. Peter's Cathedral in Rome and believes Milton had in mind anti-Catholic descriptions of the election of a pope.)

"MEN ONLY DISAGREE/OF CREATURES RATIONAL" (lines 496-505) This effective plea for peace is one of many made by Milton in *Paradise Lost*. Here, at the end of the Council scene, Milton points out that even Devils can reach concord, while men live in "hatred, enmity, and strife."

ALLEGORY OF SIN AND DEATH (lines 648-889) The basis for this allegory lies in James i, 15: "When lust hath conceived, it bringeth forth sin, and sin, when it is finished, bringeth forth death." Milton, as was his habit, has elaborated upon the Biblical line most imaginatively, adding the detail of the incest between Sin and Death.

The birth of Sin should be compared with the classical legend of the birth of Athena (Wisdom) from the head of Zeus. The description of Sin as half-woman, half-serpent should be compared with Ovid's description of Scylla (*Metamorphoses*, xiv, 70-74) and with Spenser's description of Error (*The Faerie Queene*, I, i, 14).

SATAN'S VOYAGE THROUGH CHAOS (lines 890-1040) While Milton's adaptation of the allegory of Sin and Death has met a varied critical reception, his success in giving an impression of Chaos, the indescribable, has been much commented upon. Note particularly how in lines 946-950 his meter (with its repeated use of spondees) suggests Satan's struggle as he makes his way through the abyss of Chaos and Night, where only Chance

> So eagerly the fiend
> O'er bog or steep, through strait, rough, dense, or rare,
> With head, hands, wings, or feet pursues his way,
> And swims or sinks, or wades, or creeps, or flies . . .

BOOK III This book can be divided into a number of distinct sections. The first fifty-five lines, the famous "Prologue to Light" or "Invocation to Light," serve as a transition as the scene of the epic is shifted to Heaven. The next section (lines 56-216) gives much of the theology underlying the poem: God's plans for man. His prescience of Adam's Fall, His willingness that repentant men be saved if anyone in Heaven will offer the perfect atonement. (The fallen angels sinned without temptation and therefore are justly damned; but man will sin only through being led astray by Satan and so deserves the possibility of a lesser punishment.) The Son of God offers himself as the atonement (lines 227 ff.), and the angels sing of their great joy in a hymn of praise of the Father and Son (lines 344 ff.).

The scene then shifts to Satan on his journey to find God's new creation, man. The Devil reaches the outer rim of the universe, passes through Limbo or the Paradise of Fools (lines 400 ff.), gets as far as the Gate of Heaven, then goes to the Orb of the Sun. Spying the archangel Uriel, the Regent of the Sun (lines 654 ff.), Satan disguises himself as a young or lesser angel and is able to learn from Uriel the location of the Garden of Eden. The Satan-Uriel scene is made use of by Milton to show his scorn of hypocrisy (lines 681 ff.) and his acknowledgment that only God can recognize this most detestable of sins; he also has the deceived Uriel praise the spirit of research and investigation, even into God's acts, that he thinks his questioner is showing.

COMMENTARY

CHARACTERS   God, the Son of God; Uriel; Satan.

SETTING   The two scenes that are important in the devlopment of the epic take place in Heaven and on the Orb of the Sun. The reader also follows Satan on his long journey from the gates of Hell to Light.

THE INVOCATION TO LIGHT   (lines 1-55)   This prologue is considered by many critics to be one of the most beautiful and interesting passages in *Paradise Lost*. The obvious autobiographical elements in it should not be allowed to hide its other values.

Sympathy for Milton in his affliction makes the average reader tend to think of all references to light in direct connection with the poet's blindness. And there is no doubt that in this apostrophe Milton is writing about his physical blindness:

> but thou [the sun]
> Revisit'st not these eyes, that roll in vain
> To find thy piercing ray, and find no dawn;
> So thick a drop serene hath quencht th'ir Orbs,
> Or dim suffusion veil'd.   (lines 22-26)

On the other hand, even if the author had not been blind, this appeal to his Muse in the form of Light comes at a most fit point in the narrative: after describing Hell, that "Eternal Night" and Chaos, he is about to put the grandeur of Heaven and the infinite Goodness and Justice of God and His Son into terms understandable to man.

It should also be noted that for a man as well-read as Milton, Light had many connotations that went beyond the simple "God is light" of the Bible (I John i, 5). Dante wrote of light as God's creative power; he also uses the terminology of God as "the spiritual and intellectual Sun." Later Italian philosophers had written about a spiritual ladder of light by which man climbed to God. Variations of the light image were, in short, fairly common in religious and philosophical writing; therefore, Milton's use of light images should be considered in relationship to this background.

In the last part of the invocation Milton sadly admits that day never returns for him, that he never sees the "Summer's Rose" nor "human face divine," that he is shut off from much learning. Then he soars in spirit to claim that therefore so much the more "Celestial Light" shines inwardly to enable him to "see and tell/ Of things invisible to mortal sight." These lines should not be interpreted only as evidence of Milton's self-esteem. They should be read with the theory in mind that great poetry and art can be created only by men who deserve and enjoy divine illumination. This belief was held by many in the Renaissance and is still with us.

GOD AND HIS SON   (lines 56-343)   Next to Milton's depiction of the War in Heaven (Book VI), this portrayal of the Father and Son in Heaven has been the most adversely criticized part of the whole epic. (Usually the Son of God is thought to be more adequately handled than the Creator.) Even critics who are inclined to deal gently with Milton's possible failures or lapses in artistic judgment have wished that the poet had had God speak only through His archangels or through His Son. But Milton's earlier readers would not have been disturbed by the passage, brought up as they were with a very anthropomorphic God, Who (in a favorite sermon image) collected the tears of the faithful in vials.

FREE WILL   (lines 93-134)   This is a basic passage for understanding *Paradise Lost* as it is God's own justification of His gift of free will to man.

THE OFFER OF REDEMPTION   (lines 217 ff.)   The whole scene in which the Son of God offers to sacrifice Himself for man should be compared with the scene in the previous book in which Satan offers to go on his mission to destroy man.

THE CHORUS OF THE ANGELS   (lines 344-415)   This passage, with its echoes of Revelation, is one of the most musical and colorful parts of the epic. In addition to their aesthetic value, these two verse paragraphs show at least three characteristics of Milton's mind: his concept that Heaven consists of perfect harmony—the angelic harps are "ever tun'd" (line 366); his habit of thinking of himself as part of any chorus of praise of the Almighty and His Son—"never shall my Harp thy praise/ Forget, nor from thy Father's praise disjoin" (lines 414-415); and, theologically, his variation from conventional Trinitarian thought—"Begotten Son, Divine Similitude" (line 384).

THE ALLEGORY OF LIMBO OR THE PARADISE OF FOOLS (lines 444-496) This allegory usually is regarded as an unnecessary intrusion into the movement of the narrative. The passage can be considered as mere anti-Catholicism, but some defense of it has been made by considering that Milton meant the types portrayed to be human equivalents of Sin and Death, all offspring of Satan.

THE LADDER TO HEAVEN (lines 510 ff.) The image is based on Jacob's ladder, Genesis xxviii, 12. Compare the Bridge from Hell to Earth in Book X, lines 272-324.

URIEL (lines 654 ff.) This angel, whose name means "God is light" or "the fire of God," is not mentioned in the Bible, but according to Hebrew tradition he was one of the four great archangels, sharing this honor with Michael, Gabriel, and Raphael.

BOOK IV The action begins with Satan nearing the Garden of Eden. In a long soliloquy (lines 32-113) he argues with himself in order to justify his proposed action: to corrupt man, God's new creation. As his evil nature takes control of him, his appearance degenerates and his actions become wild. In this state he is seen and recognized by Uriel, the angel that had allowed him to continue on his way to the Garden (Book III).

In order to spy on the newly created Garden and its inhabitants, Satan takes the form of a cormorant (a bird often used as a symbol of greed), perching on the Tree of Life near the edge of the Garden. From this spot he is able to see not only the beauty of Eden but the charming pair, Adam and Eve. Such is the attractiveness of the happy two that Satan almost is moved to give up his project, but convinces himself (in another soliloquy, lines 357-392) that he must continue with his evil plot in order to hold his position in Hell.

So that he may come closer to them, the Fiend then takes the form of various animals, capering around. Unaware of the eavesdropper, Adam speaks to Eve (lines 411-439) of their gratitude to their Creator Who has given them so much, and Satan finds out about the forbidden Tree of Knowledge. Eve replies (lines 440-491), revealing her simplicity and her vanity. The Devil becomes even more jealous of their pleasure in each other. In the meantime, Uriel reports to Gabriel, who is in command of the angels guarding Paradise, and the latter promises to have the intruder found (lines 560 ff.).

Night is now approaching, and the scene shifts back to Adam and Eve. Adam explains to Eve the seeming contradiction that nighttime is very beautiful but it is the proper or normal time to sleep. They pray in unison (lines 720 ff.) and retire together, to enjoy their marital joy naturally and without hypocrisy.

Gabriel sends three angels, Uzziel, Ithuriel, and Zephon, to protect the Garden with its young couple from the reported intruder. Ithuriel and Zephon surprise Satan, in the form of a toad, at Eve's ear, corrupting her by a dream (lines 799 ff.). They bring him to Gabriel. Satan then shows his powers of deception by trying to outwit Gabriel (lines 885 ff.). First the fallen angel claims that he escaped from Hell merely to avoid more suffering; then he shifts to the argument that he has been on an innocent voyage of discovery. But Gabriel, with his God given reason, cannot be deceived.

The war between the faithful and the rebellious angels almost breaks out again, but the sight of the constellation Libra (the Scales of Justice), lowered into visibility by God, makes Satan decide to depart.

COMMENTARY

CHARACTERS   Uriel, Gabriel, Uzziel, Ithuriel, Zephon; Adam and Eve; Satan.

SETTING   This book is centered upon the Garden of Eden, but at times the angels protecting it are outside the Garden proper.

SATAN'S SOLILOQUY   (lines 32-113)   The first lines (32-39) are those that Edward Phillips, the poet's nephew, said Milton wrote as early as 1642, planning to use them as the opening of a drama on the Fall of man.

This soliloquy in its portrayal of Satan's changing moods and his honesty with himself brings to mind the great Shakespearean soliloquies. The fallen angel admits that he owed gratitude to his Creator but he "understood not that a grateful mind/ By owing owes not" (lines 55-56). He wonders whether his high position in heaven had not been his undoing, but decides that he would have fallen anyway by joining forces with some other rebellious Power. He questions whether he had had the same free will as the other angels, but he has to acknowledge that he had. At the depth of his despondency—"Which way I fly is Hell; myself am Hell" (line 75)—he considers repentance, but pride and shame before his followers forbid it; anyway, if he went back to God's fold, he would have only a "worse relapse,/ And heavier fall" (line 101).

> So farewell Hope, and with Hope farewell Fear,
> Farewell Remorse: all Good to me is lost;
> Evil be thou my Good . . .   (lines 108-110)

He will try to have in man at least "Divided Empire" with "Heav'n's King" (line 111).

EPIC SIMILE   (line 183 ff.)   This effective description of Satan is based on a New Testament line, John x, 1. Note epic (or Homeric) simile construction:

> As when a prowling Wolf,
> Whom hunger drives . . .
> Leaps o'er the fence with ease into the Fold:
> Or as a Thief bent to unhoard the cash
> Of some rich Burgher . . .
> In at the window climbs, or o'er the tiles:
> So clomb this first grand Thief into God's Fold . . .

PARADISE OR THE GARDEN OF EDEN   (lines 208-287, 340-352, 624-632; see also Book V, lines 291-297, and Book IX, lines 205-212)   Marjorie Nicolson (*Milton*) believes that Milton's description of Paradise should be read in the light of a controversy that was interesting Englishmen as early as the seventeenth century and certainly was an issue in more Romantic periods: How much should nature be controlled? Should gardens (and landscaping) appear natural, or should they be works of art, nature "improved"? Milton straddles the two points of view admirably. Adam and Eve apparently believed in a middle course, contenting themselves (at least until they had children of a working age) with lopping "wanton growth" and getting rid of fallen blossoms and gums (resin).

ADAM AND EVE   (lines 287 ff.)   Milton's Adam and Eve in their unfallen state have great beauty:

> *Adam* the goodliest man of men since born
> His Sons, the fairest of her Daughters *Eve*.

Following classical tradition that can be traced back to Plato, the poet stressed their uprightness, in symbolic comparison with the rest of creation. (See also Book VII, lines 506 ff.). Also of interest is Milton's carefully drawn distinction between the sexes: In both "the image of their glorious Maker shone," but they are not "equal"—

> For contemplation hee and valor form'd,
> For softness shee and sweet attractive Grace,
> Hee for God only, shee for God in him . . .

SATAN'S SECOND SOLILOQUY   (lines 358-393, 505-535)   The soliloquy is broken by the description of Adam and Eve as Satan spies upon them in the Garden. Technically, this allows Satan to discover at this crucial time, that they have been forbidden to eat the fruit of the Tree of Knowledge, and so he learns his means of attack.

The Devil is almost moved by their "harmless innocence," but his pity gives way to his desire for revenge and his need to maintain his position in Hell (the "Tyrant's plea"). Finally envy overpowers him.

EVE'S CREATION   (lines 449 ff.)   Eve's recollection of the events that immediately followed her creation should be compared with Adam's narrative, Book VIII, lines 249 ff.

In one sense Eve seems to be the completely innocent woman becoming aware of herself and giving herself naturally to man. There is, however, a decided suggestion of ominous vanity in Eve's account of looking at her image in a pond, especially as the scene recalls the old story of Narcissus and his falling in love with his reflected image.

GABRIEL   (lines 549 ff.)   Traditionally, Gabriel, the "man of God," is one of man's protecting or guardian angels, but Milton had no Biblical basis for assigning him the special guardianship of Eden.

IDEAL MARRIAGE   (lines 741 ff.)   Here Milton gives his concept of what "wedded love" should be like, without prudery or artificial chivalry.

UZZIEL   (lines 782 ff.)   Uzziel, "the strength of God," is an example of Milton's use for an angel of a name that is to be found in the Bible, but only as a man's name.

ITHURIEL   (lines 788 ff.)   The name means "discovery of God" and is not in the Bible.

ZEPHON   (lines 788 ff.)   The name means "searcher" and is in the Bible, but as a man's name.

THE DISCOVERY OF SATAN IN THE FORM OF A TOAD AT EVE'S EAR   (lines 797 ff.)   This is a very dramatic version of an old tradition that Eve was twice tempted.

In Satan's consequent disputes first with Ithuriel and Zephon, then with Gabriel, the Archfiend's pride and rage seem overwhelming, but at the sight of the Scales of Justice he flees "murmuring," very much the coward.

THE SCALES OF JUSTICE   (lines 997 ff.)   The sudden lowering of the Scales of Justice by God at the crucial moment seems to modern readers a very artificial conclusion to the book, but Milton had a number of classical precedents for the concept.

BOOK V This book is one of the most easily read parts of *Paradise Lost*. It is also one of the most interesting parts as it reveals much of Milton's thinking.

The book opens just after the first temptation of Eve. Satan, squatting beside her like a toad (a symbol of evil), has caused her to dream of the pleasures of tasting the fruit of the forbidden tree. When Adam awakens her, she tells him of this confusing experience. He reassures her, and in so doing makes a number of philosophical and psychological points: We are not responsible for the evil that passes through our minds as long as our reason rejects it. Reason is man's highest faculty, to which the other faculties—imagination, fancy, etc.—are subservient ("faculty" psychology).

Adam and Eve leave their shelter to start their day with prayer (lines 136 ff.). This beautiful passage, based on Psalm CXLVIII, has as its theme that all nature worships the Creator. As they are praying, God is moved by pity to send one of His archangels, Raphael, to tell them about the fall of the angels and that Satan is about to tempt them, too, to fall. As they have free will, a doctrine about angels and men stressed again and again by Milton, the forewarning also makes man's progenitors fully responsible for their Fall.

Raphael's splendor is seen afar by the two inhabitants of the Garden. In a light, amusing passage Eve prepares for their distinguished guest. When the archangel joins them, there necessarily follows a consideration of the nature of angels (lines 403 ff.): Not only are angels like men, only vastly superior, but there is no sharp distinction between spirit and matter. Therefore Raphael can partake of the feast of fruit that Eve has selected for him.

At Adam's request, Raphael prepares to spend the afternoon explaining the reason for man's creation (lines 563 ff.). This point (or line 577, the actual start of Raphael's tale) is the chronological beginning of the poem. Following standard epic pattern, the opening part of the action, the first cause of the tragedy, is thus supplied slightly before the halfway mark of the whole poem. In *Paradise Lost*, at this point too, the reader is given Milton's necessary philosophical assumption: Spiritual facts can only be depicted in material form. Hence what has happened in Heaven can only be worded in terms that would apply to Earth.

Raphael tells his tale in a semidramatic form, letting his "characters"—God, the Son of God, Satan, Abdiel—each speak for himself. God elevates His Son above the other inhabitants of Heaven. One archangel, from then on nameless in Heaven but known on Earth and in Hell as Satan, feels that his superior position is being threatened. He manages (using trickery) to call a council of such angels as he hopes will join him in rebellion. He easily sways the group gathered, one third of the angels in Heaven, to follow him. Nevertheless, one seraph, Abdiel (lines 803 ff.) nobly refuses to be one with them. Thus Milton is able to show his concept of true courage, the assertion of the truth by an individual in the face of the mob.

COMMENTARY

CHARACTERS   God and His Son, Raphael, Adam and Eve; Satan; Abdiel.

SETTING   Most of Book V, except for the commissioning of Raphael by God to instruct Adam and Eve, actually takes place in the Garden of Eden, first with Adam and Eve as a happy pair and then with Raphael talking to them. Once the archangel starts his tale, however, the action—and interest—shifts to Heaven before the Creation of man.

EVE'S DREAM   Some critics feel that when Eve dreams of the pleasures of sin, then sin has entered Eden, and so the Fall of mankind has occurred.

Others hold that Adam's exoneration of Eve from any blame in dreaming of evil should be accepted: Evil may enter our minds through our imagination or fancy, but we do not sin if reason expels the evil concept. Certainly Milton speaks of Eve as still sinless after the dream.

If the dream is accepted as the downfall of Eve, another question is raised. Is it fair that Eve should be corrupted while asleep? This questioning of God's justice has been answered by suggesting that the evil had to be present in Eve's mind or she would not have dreamed as she did. Such psychological arguments surely go beyond the version of the Fall that Milton is seeking to give.

Even if the dream is accepted merely as the opening step in Eve's downfall, in the sense that it has aroused her desires, the later scene (Book IX, lines 205-384) in which she persuades Adam to allow her to be alone, unprotected by him from Satan, has to be read with the question of her subconscious motivation in mind. She (and Adam) remained free, however, to fall or not to fall; this point Milton stresses repeatedly.

It should be noted that both the significance of dreams and the possibility that evil spirits could attack through dreams were still very frequently debated subjects in Milton's day, as they had been for centuries.

RAPHAEL (lines 221 ff.) Raphael, whose name means "medicine of God," is one of the four great archangels of Jewish tradition. In the apocryphal Book of Tobit he accompanies and instructs Tobias on his journey. Milton suggests the archangel's kindly qualities by calling him the "sociable Spirit" and the "affable Angel." (*Affable*, carries with it the connotation, which has fallen into some disuse, of being civil and kind to one's inferiors.)

PLATONIC IDEAS Included in Raphael's instruction of Adam and Eve (and Adam's replies) are many concepts to be found in Plato, as most of Milton's contemporary readers would recognize. Note particularly lines 329-333 and 571-576, in which Adam is told that the laws of Heaven and Earth are the same and that the Earth is a shadow of Heaven; lines 415-426, Raphael's explanation of the four elements passing into one another; lines 488-490, the distinction between intuition and reasoning; lines 509-512, "By steps we may ascend to God" (the Scale of Nature); and lines 620 ff., the orderly movement of the stars in a sort of "mystical dance."

BOOK VI Raphael continues his account of what took place in Heaven before the creation of man. (It should be noted that parts of this book have been severely censured by many critics.)

Abdiel, having left the rebellious angels (Book V, lines 803 ff.), is taken back into God's fold, with welcoming words as the ideal servant of God (lines 29 ff.).

Before the general battle between the loyal angels (under Gabriel and Michael) and the attacking forces (under Satan and a number of lesser chieftains), Abdiel and Satan face each other in single combat. In the verbal clash between the two that precedes the dual, Abdiel nobly defines the difference between service and servitude (lines 174-181). Then Abdiel succeeds in severely wounding Satan, but the latter retains enough of his angel nature to recover immediately. (Devils can suffer but not be destroyed.)

The war in Heaven follows (lines 202 ff.). The first day Satan's followers are hard-pressed, and that night they invent gunpowder (lines 469 ff.). The second day, however, they seem for a time to be successful; Satan is full of glee as he feels victory is his. But when organized warfare fails, the loyal angels resort to throwing mountains and the rebellious angels retaliate in kind. (Presumably Milton is showing that no type of warfare, such as is practiced in any age, from single combat to massive action, leads to anything but confusion and utter destruction.)

God then sends His Son to rout Satan's forces. In a symbolic chariot (based on Ezekiel I), the Messiah forcefully drives them through Chaos to Hell. (With lines 864-877 the action that took place before the opening of the epic has been completed—cf. Book I, lines 44-49.) The Son then returns to the throne of God, where he "now sits at the right hand of bliss."

The book concludes with one more warning from Raphael: Adam should profit from learning the results of disobedience (lines 893-912).

COMMENTARY

CHARACTERS Raphael, Adam and Eve. In Raphael's account of the battle in Heaven: God and His Son, Abdiel, Michael, Gabriel, Uriel, Raphael, Zophiel; Satan, Belial, Moloch, Nisroc, Ariel, and lesser devils.

SETTING The story is told in the Garden of Eden. The main action of Raphael's account is in Heaven, except for rout of Satan and his followers to Hell.

ABDIEL As in Book V, Milton seems to be giving Abdiel the qualities that he himself most admired, the points of character that he felt himself to possess. God commends the courageous angel in the highest terms:

> Servant of God, well done, well hast thou fought
> The better fight, who single hast maintain'd
> Against revolted multitude the Cause
> Of Truth, in word mightier than they in Arms.
>
> (lines 29-32)

Milton is also giving his own views, as expressed in his prose, when he distinguishes between service and servitude. Abdiel answers Satan's objection to worshipping God and accepting His mandates:

Apostate, still thou err'st . . .
Unjustly thou deprav'st it with the name
Of *Servitude* to serve whom God ordains,
Or Nature; God and Nature bid the same,
When he who rules is worthiest, and excels
Them whom he governs. This is servitude,
To serve th' unwise, or him who hath rebell'd
Against his worthier, as thine now serve thee,
Thyself not free, but to thy self enthrall'd.

(lines 172-181)

In these lines we can see Milton as the man who used his pen in defense of the execution of an unworthy king and the assumption of power by Cromwell.

THE WAR in HEAVEN   Both at the beginning and the end of his tale Raphael carefully explains to Adam that the "high matter" involved has to be made understandable by "lik'ning spiritual to corporal forms" (Book V, line 573) and by "measuring things in Heav'n by things on Earth" (Book VI, line 893). Nevertheless, there has been much criticism of the confusion between spirit and matter; for many readers the War in Heaven approaches the ridiculous. Spirits are handicapped by their armor. Spirits invent gunpowder, which they use against other spirits. It should be noted, of course, that the invention of cannons and gunpowder, while it may seem more anachronistic, is not very different from the use of armor and swords in Heaven and Hell (and this Milton has depicted throughout his epic) or from the finding of precious stones in Hell and building of Pandaemonium, described so vividly in Book I.

But in trying to respond with horror to the tremendous events of the War in Heaven, the reader is put under an additional strain. He must face with Milton the very difficult task of keeping interest in a war in which no participant can be permanently injured or killed. Nor in the larger sense can there be any dramatic suspense: the success of the virtuous, those on God's side, is not to be doubted.

Considering the difficulties of any attempt to be at all specific about a War in Heaven, Milton's defenders have noted that his failures to be impressive are relatively few; then, too, the action moves so rapidly that the whole effect is remarkably overwhelming.

IRONY   In the early eighteenth century one passage in this book, lines 609-628, was considered by Addison to be extremely offensive, and this adverse criticism has been repeated with some frequency. The lines under question, an exchange of pleasantries between Satan and Belial, come immediately after the angels fall back in confusion when first attacked by the "thunder" of the newly invented cannons. In their glee at their apparent victory, the two Fiends jibe at the plight of the seraphim and outdo each other in punning at their victims' expense.

Addison obviously disliked the intrusion of a light or witty note into the tragic War in Heaven; many modern readers, perhaps less impressed with the grandeur of the War, will not be offended by the change in tone. In judging the passage, moreover, two points should be kept in mind. First, plays upon words were much more acceptable in the seventeenth century than in later ages; in fact, what we now somewhat contemptuously term "punning" used to be regarded as an interesting exercise of mind or knowledge. Secondly, the rejoining of Satan and Belial in what they think is their victory, without sorrow for their injured opponents, is indicative of their degenerated natures; as Devils, they can taunt their erstwhile companions, now thought to be defeated.

CHARIOT OF PATERNAL DEITY   (lines 749 ff.)   The chariot is based on the first chapter of Ezekiel. A repetition of the concept is to be seen in Book VII, lines 218 ff., but without as much color and detail.

BOOK VII This book begins (lines 1-39), as did Book I, with an invocation to Urania, the "Heav'nly Muse." Having reached the midpoint in his epic, Milton again asks for help from a power greater than himself that he may be able to represent adequately the great events of his story. In this apostrophe to Urania he permits himself a brief personal allusion to his blindness and other difficulties, as he had in the Invocation to Light, the opening lines of Book III.

The narrative proper resumes with Adam asking Raphael about events after the expulsion of the rebellious angels and the creation of the new universe. The archangel consents to give Adam more knowledge about God's decision to create man to take the place of the fallen angels.

The story of Creation (lines 255 ff.) is based, of course, primarily on the first chapter of Genesis, with some modification (notably the agency of the Son of God) from the New Testament. But Milton does far more than paraphrase the biblical version. The Son of God, with his Father's overshadowing Spirit and might, rides forth in his chariot to create the universe from chaos; here there is an implied contrast with Satan's journey through Chaos to destroy man. As Raphael continues to instruct Adam, many details are added to the stark simplicity of Genesis. Milton makes use of points the Church fathers had discussed as possibilities: for example, the question of whether mountains are balanced by depths in the oceans. He brings in Galilean astronomy (lines 364-366, 375-378, 574-578). He puts more stress on the closely connected and rising order (the "chain of being") of creation: lowly plants, grass, herbs, trees; fish, dolphins, whales; little birds, eagles; and finally man, God's masterwork because of his power to reason.

According to the Old Testament, the world was created in six days, with the seventh day one of rest. Raphael explains that this day of rest was devoted to musical praise of the Creator by all the angels in Heaven. Thus the book ends with a magnificent hymn (lines 602 ff.) extolling God in his formation of Good after the destruction of Evil.

COMMENTARY

CHARACTERS   Raphael, Adam and Eve; God, the Son of God, angels as a chorus.

SETTING   Raphael's instructive tale still is being told in the Garden of Eden. The action of his account starts in Heaven (with the decision to create man) and ends in the Garden of Eden with the creation of Adam. Then the scene is shifted back to Heaven for the choir of angels to sing their praise of the Creator.

INVOCATION TO URANIA   (lines 1-39)   Milton asks for continued help from Urania as the "Heav'nly Muse" (that is, from heaven) that he may still sing

> unchang'd
> To hoarse or mute, though fall'n on evil days,
> On evil days though fall'n, and evil tongues;
> In darkness, and with dangers compast round,
> And solitude . . .

This pathetic appeal (lines 24-28) comes as near self-pity as Milton ever allows himself, but note that his concern is for his great work, not for himself. The passage is often used to date his writing of Book VII, and by implication the remaining books of the epic. Presumably he composed these lines soon after the Restoration, some time in 1661 when he was in decided danger of suffering long imprisonment because of his support of Cromwell, his holding office under the Commonwealth, and his defense of the execution of Charles I.

THE CREATION STORY   (lines 205-547)   It must be remembered that the Creation has been a favorite subject of many writers and artists. Milton could gather suggestions for details from various sources. One version that he certainly knew was DuBartas' *La Première Semaine* and *La Seconde Semaine*, translated into English by Joshua Sylvester as *DuBartas His Divine Weeks and Works* (1592-1595), an interpretation of Genesis that influenced many religious writers in the seventeenth century and was particularly popular in Puritan circles.

Milton's depiction of Creation is remarkable in two aspects: First, he manages to convey the idea of movement, of action. Neither plants nor animals are just there; all come to life as each part of the created world moves distinctively. The "Stately trees" "rose as in a Dance" (line 324); birds fly (line 389); schools of fish "with their Finns and shining Scales/ Glide under the green Wave" (lines 400-402); the huge whale stretches itself (lines 413 ff.); eagles and storks build their treetop nests (lines 423-465); the elephant "upheav'd/ His vastness" (lines 471-472). Milton's second outstanding accomplishment in telling the Creation story is the sense of harmony that he conveys in a scene that with all its action might become mere confusion. His firm belief in a rising scale in an ordered universe is clear. Supposedly this harmony in the Garden of Eden is symbolized by the music Adam hears as he is created.

GOLDEN COMPASSES (line 225) In considering this image and its repeated use by many different writers, the reader must remember that the word *compass* was often used in the sense of *circle*. The effective figure of the Creator using a compass or circle in laying out the universe is to be found in the Bible (Proverbs viii, 27) as well as in Dante and many other writers. Donne, too, has a noted compass image.

HYMN OF PRAISE (lines 602 ff.) This magnificent paean is based on psalms of thanksgiving (including Psalms VIII, IX, XIV, XXIV) and passages in Revelation. The hymn as Milton has constructed it is far more than conventional praise of God. The angels in praising Jehovah as "greater now in thy return/ Than from [the casting out of] the Giant Angels" are expressing the philosophic idea that it is always better to create than to destroy. The Creation story could have no more fitting conclusion.

BOOK VIII Adam next asks Raphael, the "Divine Historian," for an explanation of the construction of the universe. Eve leaves (lines 41 ff.). Raphael's reply offers two alternatives: the older (Ptolemaic) theory of the earth as the center about which the other planets revolve; and the newer theories (Copernican and Galilean) in which the planets, including the earth, revolve around the sun (lines 66-178). Then the archangel warns Adam not to waste time in speculation about the unknowable, but to be "lowly wise" in concentrating on the immediate problem of resisting Satan.

Adam thanks his Heaven-sent mentor and offers to tell him of his creation. Raphael, who had been occupied in the rout of Satan at the time, becomes in turn a willing listener.

The narrative (lines 249 ff.) that follow expands the second chapter of Genesis in a number of ways. Adam becomes aware of himself and of the charm of his surroundings; falling asleep, he has a vision of his Creator, Who shows him the world He has created for him. He wakes to find that the Guide of his dream is with him. He is told that all this beautiful world is for his use and pleasure, with the exception of the Tree of Knowledge. The prohibition and penalties for disobedience are clearly worded (lines 323-333). Adam then names the fish, birds, and animals—the birds and beasts coming before him two by two and indicating their subservience to him.

But Adam is not satisfied with his world, for there is no happiness in solitude. God teases him a bit that man has the lower forms of creation for company and that the Divinity does not need such a helpmate. Adam, however, is wisely firm that man needs rational companionship. God is not at all displeased. Consequently, while Adam is in a trance, Eve, his "other self," is created (lines 453-499). The first man proves to be a very loving husband. As he admits, his love of Eve overrules his understanding that she is his inferior in "mind/And inward Faculties"; in fact, "what she wills to do or say,/Seems wisest, virtuousest, discreetest, best" (lines 541-550). This obvious adulation of Eve is quickly rebuked by Raphael. Man must maintain his dignity and not allow passion to rule his reason. (The necessity for this warning serves as preparation for the coming temptation and Fall of Adam.)

Adam has one more question: How do angels love? Raphael, blushing, assures him that angels do love (or there would be no happiness in Heaven). Their communion is not restricted by bodily barriers, as is the case with man and women. Refusing to be more explicit, Raphael gives Adam one last warning to obey God's commands and not let passion overcome his free will.

COMMENTARY

CHARACTERS   Raphael; Adam and Eve.

SETTING   Garden of Eden.

STRUCTURE   Books VII and VIII originally (1667 edition) were one long book. When Milton for the 1674 edition divided VII to make two books of it, he added the first four lines of the present VIII.

EVE'S LEAVING   (lines 40-63)   Eve leaves to tend her plants, but according to Milton she is capable of understanding Raphael (lines 49-50). She simply prefers to get her knowledge mixed with Adam's caresses. Milton approves of her attitude, but she does not seem guileless even though she may be guiltless.

THE "TERRESTIAL MOON"   (lines 140-152)   The possibility that other planets might be inhabited was a natural sequitur to the Copernican theory of many planets revolving around the sun. Here Milton raises—but does not have the archangel answer—the question of whether or not the moon is so inhabited, a question that has intrigued many generations.

"BE LOWLY WISE"   (lines 167-175)   Raphael is really stressing moderation: Adam should be inquisitive and seek knowledge, but he should not spend his time dreaming of "other Worlds." (It was standard Puritan dogma that man could not know all, or he would equal God; if he tried to equal God, he was, of course, guilty of the sin of pride.)

ADAM'S PASSION   (lines 528 ff.)   Adam naively admits to Raphael the effect Eve has upon him: He finds himself weak/ "Against the charm of Beauty's powerful glance" (lines 532-533). Eve seems "wisest, virtuousest, discreetest, best"; her loveliness is so "absolute" that all his higher knowledge is "degraded," his wisdom "discount'nanc't" (lines 546-559). Raphael in reply rebukes him by reminding him that carnal love is given to both men and animals; true love, with its seat in Reason, approaches heavenly love (lines 561-594). But Adam, after the way of lovers, denies that his love is limited; he feels that he and Eve have "Union of Mind, or in us both one Soul" (line 604).

Adam's admission of his overpowering passion clearly indicates the cause of his Fall (Book IX). Modern readers find Adam's adulation of Eve pleasing, but any seventeenth-century man at all religious-minded would be well aware of Adam's closeness to sin in that he might put his love of his wife before his love of (and duty to) his God; for Milton the danger lay particularly in the threatened abrogation of Reason, God's greatest gift to man.

BOOK IX Traditionally, in Book IX the epic reaches its climax with Adam and Eve actually eating the forbidden fruit of the Tree of Knowledge. Modern criticism, with its emphasis on psychology, has pointed out that Eve may be said to have fallen when she had her dream of evil (Book IV, lines 799-899 and Book V, lines 1-135) and was so disturbed by it, for she then knew good from evil; and Adam had already fallen when he admitted (Book VIII, lines 530-559) that his passion for Eve overcame his superior masculine reason. (The interpolation of Raphael's narrative makes the time elapsed from Eve's first temptation to the second seem longer than it really is—see Book IX, lines 53-69.) Tillyard, a very sensitive modern English critic, held that the Fall continues after the actual deed and that the climax of *Paradise Lost* comes in Book X (lines 720 ff.) when Adam admits his guilt, accepts the justice of man's punishment, forgives Eve, and in his repentance turns back to God—the predicted good has come out of evil.

Book IX begins with another invocation by Milton to his "Celestial Patroness," for the poet now has the sad task of telling how Sin, Death, and suffering came into the world (lines 1-47).

The narrative returns to Satan. Driven away once by the angels protecting the Garden, the Fiend returns. In a soliloquy (lines 99-178) he shows his degeneration: He no longer seeks to alleviate his own misery; he wants to make others as miserable as he is. He knows revenge soon becomes bitter, but he wants it anyway. And he admits his envy of "this new Favorite/ Of Heav'n" (lines 175-176).

After morning prayers, Eve proposes that she and Adam separate for the morning so that they will get more of their gardening done (lines 205-225). Adam admires her proposed diligence, but points out that the Creator meant man to have some pleasure also; furthermore, he fears that Satan will take advantage of her being alone to try her virtue (lines 226-268). Eve is insulted that he doubts her ability to stand alone (lines 273-289). Adam is apologetic—he does not mean to doubt her, but there is more strength in unity (lines 290-317). She still persists, "sweetly": Are they always to live in fear? And what are "Faith, Love, Virtue" unless tried (lines 322-341)? Adam responds with a little lecture on free will (lines 343-356): Danger lies within man. Temptation should not be sought (line 364). And then "domestic *Adam*" breaks down and gives her permission to leave (lines 372-375). They part tenderly.

Satan, spying Eve alone, is so overcome by her beauty that for the moment he is "stupidly good" (line 465), but he soon rejoices in his opportunity to corrupt her while she is unprotected by her husband. "Enclos'd/ In

Serpent," he approaches her and starts to flatter her. She is properly surprised at his ability to speak (lines 533-566). He tells her of a wonderful fruit he has eaten which gave him reason; with reason, came his great admiration of Eve (lines 568-612). Eve knows she is being flattered but consents to go with him to the tree that bears this fruit. On seeing that it is the Tree of Knowledge, she draws back in virtue (lines 647-654). But the Tempter continues: If by eating the fruit he has become as man, she, the "Queen of [the] Universe," can become a goddess (lines 681-732). Eve persuades herself she should try the fruit (lines 745-779). She eats, and "all [is] lost" (lines 780-784).

Once she has disobeyed and fallen, her other sins follow fast. She "ingorg'd without restraint" (greed); she prays to the Tree, with God becoming "our great Forbidder" (idolatry); she considers hiding her act from Adam so that she will become his superior (selfishness and pride); only her fear of being punished with death makes her decide to tell Adam, for she would have him die too and not live to enjoy Paradise with any other created woman (murder and envy) (lines 790-834).

Eve returns to Adam, tells him of the wondrous fruit and her deed. He is horrified, but decides he cannot live without her. "Against his better knowledge, not deceiv'd./ But fondly overcome with Female charm" (lines 998-999), he, too, eats the forbidden fruit.

Adam and Eve promptly indulge themselves sexually (lines 1034 ff.). But they wake in "guilty shame," symbolized by their awareness that they are naked. Adam accuses Eve of undoing them. She claims that the calamity is his fault—he should not have allowed her to go forth unprotected (lines 1144-1161) and, furthermore, he had joined her in eating. He then accuses her of ingratitude in that she does not appreciate his joining her in death (lines 1163-1189). On this note of mutual abuse the book ends.

COMMENTARY

CHARACTERS   Adam and Eve; Satan.

SETTING   Garden of Eden.

THE PROLOGUE   (lines 1-47) This invocation is often cited for its autobiographical information. The poet notes that he had been long in choosing his subject and that he had rejected the matter of chivalry for his great poem. He has faith that his "Celestial Patroness" (the "Heav'nly Muse" and Urania of other invocations) will aid him in completing *Paradise Lost*, although he admits that his own advanced age, the troubled times he is living in, and the old theory that great epics will be produced only in warm climates, are all against his enterprise.

SATAN'S DENIAL THAT GOD CREATED THE ANGELS   (lines 146-148) Elsewhere Satan takes for granted that God created the angels, who therefore owe him gratitude (Book IV, line 43). Occasionally, in his passion, he claims that angels are self-created (cf. Book I, lines 116-117 and Book V, lines 853-863). Such statements can be considered part of his heresy.

THE TREE OF PROHIBITION (lines 644-645) The symbolism of the forbidden Tree of Knowledge and the whole story of the Fall gain clarity if the reader keeps in mind that knowledge of good comes only from knowing evil.

SATAN'S DECEPTION OF EVE (lines 681-732) Many of the arguments that Satan used to persuade Eve are to be found in old Jewish legends—for example, he, the Serpent, had not died from eating the fruit, therefore she would not; that God forbade the Tree only to keep men low and ignorant.

"SO SAYING, HER RASH HAND IN EVIL HOUR . . . PLUCK'D . . ." (lines 780-784) These lines were long considered the central lines of the epic.

ADAM'S WREATH (lines 892 ff.) The fading of the wreath that Adam picked to welcome Eve home is perhaps doubly symbolic. When Eve ate the forbidden fruit, all Nature fell with her:

> Earth felt the wound, and Nature from her seat
> Sighing through all her Works gave signs of woe,
> That all was lost.   (lines 782-784)

Eve's changing relationship with Adam is also suggested as his "slack hand" drops the wreath intended for the "fairest of Creation."

ADAM'S FALL (lines 896 ff.) In the opening lines of *Paradise Lost*, Milton states that he will tell of "Man's First Disobedience" and the consequent loss of Eden till "one greater Man/ Restore us." The following epic is complete in itself: Adam disobeys, but learns through Michael's foretelling of the future that man will be redeemed by the Son of God, the Christ incarnate (Book XII, lines 358-465) *Paradise Regained* does not treat the final sacrifice of man's Saviour; the shorter epic confines itself to Christ's steadfast, reasoned resistance to Satan's tempting of Him in the wilderness, in contrast to Adam's (and Eve's) quick, passion-ridden Fall.

BOOK X In contrast with the other books, Book X consists of a series of short scenes or episodes, with the reader forced to shift his attention rapidly from one thread of the story to another. In the first lines of the book, however, Milton once more justifies God in his punishment of Adam and Eve by repeating that man had had the strength to repel Satan but fell of his own free will.

The story then proceeds with the reporting of the Fall in Heaven (lines 17 ff.). The Creator absolves the guardian angels of blame for their seeming failure to protect Adam and Eve. He then sends His Son to pass judgment on the guilty pair.

The Son descends in his glory to the Garden, but celestial visitors are now as much feared as they had been welcomed in happier days. He is forced to summon Adam and Eve. Adam tells of their disobedience; he blames Eve, but excuses his attempted shifting of the guilt by stating the fact that God of course will know the truth anyway. Eve simply confesses herself as having been beguiled by the Serpent into eating the forbidden fruit.

Having heard their statements, the Son rebukes Adam for not having asserted his proper character as the leader of the two; he did not have to follow Eve into sin (lines 144-154). Then Judgment (based on Genesis iii) is passed on the Serpent, Eve, and Adam (lines 163 ff.). Eve will bring forth her children in suffering and must submit absolutely to her husband's will. Adam must toil for his living and know that after this life he will return to the dust from which he had been taken. Then, in mercy, the Son clothes the two naked creatures before him.

With the Son of God's verdict that man will now suffer death serving as preparations for what follows, the scene now shifts (lines 229 ff.) to Sin and Death at the Gates of Hell (cf. Book II, lines 645 ff.). Continuing his allegory of Sin and Death as the beloved offspring of Satan, Milton then describes how the two build a causeway (or bridge) between Hell and Earth (lines 272-324).

Satan, still rejoicing over his double triumph, his corruption of Eve and the latter's corruption of Adam, is attempting to flee to Hell from the judgment of the Son of God. Well pleased by the new connection between Hell and Earth, the Devil speeds its builders on their way to Earth; he then uses the causeway for his own descent to Pandaemonium (lines 410 ff.). On his return to his cohorts, he boasts of his accomplishment, but the expected acclamation is turned to hisses as all, leader and followers, are turned into serpents and snakes (lines 514-523), a form, Milton explains, that many believe Devils are forced to assume for their humiliation on certain days of the year.

In the meantime, Sin and Death begin to devastate Earth. Watching these "Dogs of Hell," God (lines 616 ff.) reassures his angels that in due time His Son will conquer them. Then He arranges for the seasons to shift (lines 649 ff.). and life to become more difficult on Earth. At the same time, Discord (lines 706 ff.), the daughter of Sin, causes all the animals, birds, and fishes to war with each other. (The Decay of Nature after the Fall of Man has set in.)

Adam, seeing these changes about him but more torn by internal passion, laments his fate (lines 720-862). Finally, his reason makes him admit that he shares the guilt of Eve, "that bad woman." This long soliloquy is interrupted by Eve, who in pity approaches him. He repels her (lines 867 ff.) as a serpent, a "Rib/ Crooked by nature," and a "fair defect/ Of Nature." He even delivers a little oration (lines 897 ff.) on the small chance any man has for a happy marriage with the right mate.

Eve, however, persists in her appeal for forgiveness (lines 909 ff.), showing herself most submissive and willing to ask their Creator that she bear all the punishment. Moved, Adam forgives her (lines 945 ff.). They will have, he foresees, many days in which they will need to comfort each other. Death will not be immediate for them, but they will have "a long day's dying" to increase their suffering.

Eve responds (lines 966 ff.) by proposing joint suicide so that they at least will not produce a "woeful Race." Adam refuses (lines 1013 ff.) and points out the weaknesses in her logic: self-destruction does not mean contempt for life and pleasure, but rather implies anguish at the threat of the loss of life and pleasures that are overloved. Furthermore, he reminds her (and himself), God has promised that their Seed will bruise the Serpent's (Satan's) head. The proper action for them, sinners but contrite and penitent, is to ask their Creator for guidance.

COMMENTARY

CHARACTERS   God and the Son of God, angels; Adam and Eve; Satan, Sin and Death, Discord.

SETTING   Because of the book's episodic nature, the scene changes with fair rapidity: Heaven (the report of the Fall); the Garden of Eden (the judgment of Adam and Eve); the Gates of Hell and the Bridge between Hell and Earth; Pandaemonium or Hell (the return of the temporarily triumphant Satan); Earth (the ravaging by Sin and Death); Heaven (God's reassurance that His Son will conquer Sin and Death); the Universe (changes after the Fall); the Earth (Discord takes over); the Garden of Eden (Adam and Eve realize what they have done and are contrite; Adam forgives Eve and both pray for guidance).

MANIFOLD IN SIN   (line 16)   The sin of Adam and Eve in eating the fruit was not simply one of disobedience through pride (putting themselves above their Creator), although this idea is fundamental to the whole meaning of *Paradise Lost*. In his prose *Christian Doctrine* Milton carefully delineated the sins involved: "distrust of the divine veracity . . . unbelief; ingratitude; disobedience; gluttony; in the man excessive uxoriousness, in the woman a want of proper regard for her husband; in both an insensibility to the welfare of their offspring . . . parricide, theft, invasion of the rights of others, sacrilege, deceit, presumption in aspiring to divine attributes, fraud . . . pride, and arrogance." In short, Adam and Eve deserved their punishment!

ADAM AFTER THE FALL   (lines 125-136)   This passage has been interpreted as showing that Milton tried to invest Adam after the Fall with more dignity than the Biblical account allowed him.

THE BRIDGE OR CAUSEWAY BETWEEN HELL AND EARTH   (lines 272-324)   Reaction to this part of the Sin and Death allegory offers a good example of the variety of critical opinions to be found among Milton scholars: For Pattison (*Milton*, English Men of Letters Series, 1892), the Bridge, a "clumsy," unnecessary "fiction," had a "chilling effect upon the imagination." For Tillyard (*Studies in Milton*, 1951), the Bridge is one of the "grandest" episodes in the poem; grotesque elements are necessarily there because the whole episode is a parody of God's creation of the world in Book VII. For Whiting (*Milton and This Pendant World*, 1958), the Bridge with its downward plunge to Hell is the perfect foil for the Ladder to Heaven (Book II, lines 505-525). (We fall through pride; we gain Heaven by humility.)

THE APPLES IN HELL THAT TURN INTO BITTER ASHES (lines 547-572) This passage, in which Satan and his followers are punished further (after being turned into snakes) by being frustrated as they reach seemingly thirst-quenching fruit, only to have it turn to ashes in their mouths, has brought forth almost as varied a criticism as the description of the Bridge between Earth and Hell. Some modern critics, including Waldock, regard this whole episode as approaching a comic cartoon. On the other hand, critics as diverse as Addison, the great eighteenth-century stylist, and Edith Sitwell, the modern poet and symbolist, have found Milton's picture particularly effective. (The general idea of fruit turning into ashes and so torturing the thirsty is not, of course, original with Milton, but is very old.)

ADAMS SOLILOQUY (lines 720-844) While the whole spirit of Adam's debate with himself is reminiscent of Job's despairing complaints, Milton obviously also had in mind Isaiah xlv, 9 and 10: "Woe unto him that striveth with his Maker! . . . Woe unto him that saith unto his father, What begettest thou?"

Adam argues with himself: He had not asked for life or to be placed in Eden; as he could not fulfill the obligations incurred with this bliss, it was all right for God to reduce him to dust again. But is it fair that he also has to suffer "the sense of endless woes?" Then he answers himself. He had been willing to accept the good that came with life; he must be willing to accept the bad. Besides, every son could make the same complaint to his father, "I did not ask to be born."

Rather than continue in his present suffering, Adam feels that he would welcome death, "and be Earth/ Insensible." But (and here Hamlet comes to mind) he fears that the desired complete death of body and mind will not be his. (Milton himself believed in the death of both body and soul until the Resurrection; this (unorthodox) tenet seemed to him logical as it is fundamentally the spirit that sins and not just the body.)

Adam turns his thoughts again to the other moot question: Why should future generations suffer because of his sin? And he answers himself: Because any generations proceeding from him will also be depraved in Mind and Will.

In this admission of his own guilt and of God's justice not only in punishing him with death but also in having all future generations pay the same penalty, Adam reaches the first step in bringing himself back into God's fold. For some critics this triumph of Adam's reason over passion is the

BOOK XI The preceding book ends with Adam and Eve, contrite, praying to God. Book XI accordingly begins with their prayers being heard in Heaven. The Son of God, the "great Intercessor" (line 18), indicates to God the sorrow of the fallen pair. The Father accepts their penitence; nevertheless, in justice, He repeats His command that they be banished from the Garden of Eden. The archangel Michael (lines 99 ff.) is sent to inform them, but he is to do so with as much gentleness as possible and with the added assuagement of a prophecy of the future of their seed.

On Earth in the meantime Adam continues to speak gently to Eve; any quarreling or recrimination between the two is past (lines 133 ff.). Feeling that their prayers have been heard, they are somewhat reconciled to their fate. Ironically, their one hope is to remain in the Garden. There are indications, however, that the harmony of nature is past; no longer will all living creatures live in peace with each other (lines 182 ff.). Then Adam and Eve see the approach of Michael (lines 205 ff.).

The archangel, "solemn and sublime" (very different from the "affable" Raphael), accepts Adam's greeting. Michael then informs them (lines 251 ff.) that they must leave Eden. Womanlike, Eve regrets her tenderly cared-for flowers (lines 265 ff.). Less pathetic but also moving is Adam's fear: he will no longer be near the places in which he has heard God's commands and in which he might hope for further revelations (lines 296 ff.). Michael reassures each of them: Eve will have Adam, and her native soil is where her husband is (lines 286-292); Adam need not fear, For God is everywhere in His universe (lines 335 ff.).

After putting Eve to sleep (lines 366-369), Michael takes Adam to a hill to show him the future. The prophecy that follows (lines 423 ff.)—based, of course, in its content on Genesis—is in the form of visions and first allows Adam to see Death, which in his unfallen state he did not know. The Cain and Abel story, given very briefly as if in pantomime (lines 429-447), shows him Death through violence (murder, fratricide, induced by envy). Then Adam sees Death as the horrible result of disease, brought about by a lack of temperance and moderation in life (lines 479-493). Finally he is allowed to see Death in old age a less horrifying but still distressing picture (lines 530-546).

Michael carefully points out the lesson to be learned: Live temperately and moderately (lines 531-534); neither love nor hate life (lines 553-54). The archangel next shows Adam (lines 556 ff.) the progress of mankind as shepherds, as musicians, and as discoverers and users of metals (Genesis iv, 20-22). Then the changing panorama portrays the decadence of man before the Flood, despite the good example of Enoch (lines 665 ff.). War, with all its attendant evils, gives place only to times of base immorality.

Michael continues: Wearied and sickened by man's sins, God resolves to do away with man. But there is one good man, and so the Creator will save him and his family. The Noah story follows (lines 720 ff.). The book ends, fittingly, with the Flood abating and Noah seeing God's rainbow, a pledge or covenant that the Creator will not again destroy man by flood.

COMMENTARY

CHARACTERS God and His Son; Michael; Adam and Eve. (Biblical characters—for example, Abel, Cain, and Noah—appear in visions.)

SETTING Heaven, briefly; Garden of Eden. (The visions of the future that Michael enables Adam to see have as their settings various parts of the Earth, as the Bible account indicates.)

THE SON OF GOD AS THE GREAT INTERCESSOR (line 18) This familiar doctrine is based on I John ii, 1-2, and on the prayer of Jesus, John xvii.

THE FALL OF MAN NOT TO BE COMPLETELY REGRETTED (lines 22-30) This suggestion, which Milton repeats with added religious connotations in Book XII, lines 469-478, would have been considered thoroughly unorthodox in the seventeenth century, especially in Calvinist circles. Milton, however, believed in free will; in order to exercise free will rationally, man must know good and evil. Therefore, the Fall was necessary.

"THE RULE OF NOT TOO MUCH" (line 521) The precept that too little or too much food and drink destroys health predates Aristotle (cf. *Nicomachean Ethics*, II, ii, 6).

NEITHER LOVE LIFE, NOR HATE IT (lines 553-554) Milton undoubtedly had read similar advice in Martial, Seneca, and Horace, but Milton's lines show in the simplest of language his religious convictions about accepting God's will:

> Nor love thy life, nor hate; but what thou liv'st
> Live well, how long or short permit to Heav'n.

THE PROPHECY OF THE FUTURE OF MANKIND (lines 556 ff.) Milton knew many examples in literature of the use of similar predictions, most notably the Sibyl's foreknowledge of Roman history in the sixth book of the *Aeneid*, Britomart's shorter prophecy in Spenser's *Faerie Queene*, and a long account based on the Bible in DuBartas' *Divine Weeks*.

THE HORRORS OF WAR (lines 638-710) Milton's detestation of war is very apparent in this passage.

"OF MIDDLE AGE ONE RISEN" (lines 665 ff.) Although the patriarch's name is not given, Milton is paying tribute to Enoch, a good man who "walked with God" and was translated to Heaven. (Cf. Genesis v, 2-24.)

THE FLOOD STORY (lines 728-901) Milton bases his account on

Genesis vi and vii, but he elaborates the Old Testament version with details from other sources, especially Ovid's account of the Deucalian flood (in which Deucalion, son of Prometheus, and Pyrrha, his wife, are the only survivors of a flood sent by Zeus to punish mankind).

"SO ALL SHALL TURN DEGENERATE, ALL DEPRAV'D" (lines 807 ff.) This passage is usually cited to show Milton's disgust with unethical members of his own political party.

BOOK XII In Book XII Michael continues his historical survey of Biblical times, but now the events are rapidly narrated rather than presented as visions. (The appeal is directly to Adam's—and the reader's—intellect.)

Adam learns that for a time after the Flood man maintained the strength of character shown by Noah, but soon this "Silver Age" of virtue passed. (The patriarchal period merged into the time of kings.) Nimrod, the mighty hunter, became a despot; his followers were equally wicked. As punishment God set up the Tower of Confusion (Babel), and quarreling men no longer understood each other (lines 48-62).

At this point Adam wonders how Nimrod and his followers could be such tyrants, for man has authority over birds, fish, and animals, not over his fellow men. But Michael explains that with the Fall, man's reason has been impaired and subject to his passions; without "right Reason," there can be no "true Liberty" (lines 82-101).

Michael continues: At length, wearied of men's sins and abuses of each other, God decided to select as His own one nation, descended from one faithful man, Abraham. The Abraham story (lines 106-152) is followed by that of Moses (lines 170-260), which reaches its climax with the giving of the Law on Mount Sinai.

"This act/ Shall bruise . . ." Abraham, in a sense, and very definitely Moses and Joshua (lines 310-313) are treated as types of prefigurings of Christ, and so their examples serve as a prologue to the climactic coming of Christ, the promised "Seed to bruise the head of Satan" (lines 358-371, 386-465).

Upon hearing the great news of the Redeemer, Adam again wonders whether in the larger sense the Fall had not been fortunate (lines 469-478; cf. Book XI, lines 870-878).

Michael then finishes his historical prophesy by telling of the corruption that crept into the Church after Jesus' time. Nevertheless, although those persevering in the truth may have to suffer, the Day of Judgment will come and then the Just shall have "eternal Bliss" (lines 539-551).

"Greatly instructed," Adam promises to obey and "love with fear the only God." Confident that good in the end will overcome evil, he will remember that "suffering for Truth's sake/ Is fortitude to highest victory." Finally, taught by the example of his Redeemer, the Son of God, he will know that for the faithful death is the Gate of Life (lines 552-573).

Michael, pleased by his pupil's response, in conclusion urges Adam to strengthen himself with deeds "answerable" to his new knowledge, with Faith, Virtue, Patience, Temperance, above all with Love, by some called Charity, "the soul/ Of all the rest." Then he will leave the Garden of Eden knowing that Paradise is within him (lines 574-587).

Upon waking Eve, Michael and Adam find that she, too, is soothed and reconciled. "For God is also in sleep, and Dreams advise." She is especially comforted by her knowledge that her "Promised Seed" will restore man (lines 595-624).

With Providence their guide, Adam and Eve, hand in hand, their sadness mingled with hope, leave the Garden and take their "solitary way" (lines 645-649).

COMMENTARY

CHARACTERS   Michael; Adam and Eve; Biblical characters in Michael's historical prophesy.

SETTING   The Garden of Eden.

STRUCTURE   Originally Book XII was part of Book XI; in other words, XI and XII formed the original Book X of the 1667 edition. In separating the present Book XII from the preceding book, Milton inserted the first five lines of Book XII as a transition.

BIBLICAL BASIS   In his rapid narrative, Milton goes beyond Genesis and Exodus to use parts of Numbers, Joshua, II Samuel, I Kings, II Chronicles, and Ezra in the Old Testament; also the apocryphal second Book of Maccabees.

PROTOTYPES OF CHRIST AND NEW TESTAMENT EVENTS   (lines 227-244, 291-294, 309-313, 326-330)   The use of Old Testament figures and events as foreshadowings of New Testament figures and events was commonplace in Milton's day. (This use of types, or prototypes, has been called "typological allegory," or "prefiguring," or "prefiguration," or even "figuralism.")

THE "FORTUNATE FALL" OR THE "HAPPY SIN"   (lines 469-478)   Here we have Adam's recognition of the blessings that are to come from his Fall, a paradox that the Son of God has already worded for the Creator (Book XI, lines 22-30). This peculiar mixture of tragedy and blessing was pointed out by the Church fathers and other early commentators. (St. Augustine argued that the blessings were an example of good coming from evil, and so the Fall was part of God's plan. The idea of *Felix Culpa*—the Happy Sin—has remained part of Catholic teaching.)

Note that if the Fall is not regarded as completely tragic, then *Paradise Lost* ceases to be a true tragedy. This attitude, that the epic should not be considered as tragedy, is fostered by the whole last section of Book XII, from the time that Michael tells Adam of the coming of man's Redeemer. Then, too, the poem's ending, with its element of hope, weakens the reader's final grief for man's loss of a worldly Paradise.

THE CONCLUDING LINES   (lines 946-949)   The last lines of the epic have been commented upon from a number of points of view.

Addison, writing in 1712, suggested as a minor criticism of the whole poem that Milton would have done well to omit the last two lines and so have the book end with:

> The World was all before them, where to choose
> Thir place of rest, and Providence thir guide.

Thus the reader would be saved the "anguish" of the last verses.

On the other hand, E. E. Stoll, one of the most respected critics of the first half of the twentieth century, felt that the present ending was indeed perfect, leaving the reader with a "musing, melancholy" feeling, rather than resentment of a didactic ending (*From Shakespeare to Joyce*, 1944.)

Still a third point of view was expressed in 1962 by Joseph H. Summers. This critic feels that the omission of the last two lines—

> They hand in hand with wand'ring steps and slow,
> Through Eden took thir solitary way.

would have left Adam (and the reader) without a true memory of Adam's sin and its cost to man of suffering and death. Therefore, artistically, considering the whole purpose of the poem, and theologically Milton had to include the final, sad lines. ("The Final Vision," in Louis L. Martz, ed., *Milton: A Collection of Critical Essays*, 1966.)

CRITICAL ANALYSIS

Paradise Lost contains Milton's thinking on all of the important issues of his day. Like Swift in *Gulliver's Travels* and Lewis Carroll in *Alice in Wonderland*, Milton used his fictional characters to express his own ideas. The poem, without the knowledge of events, stands by itself as a work of great artistic beauty, but knowledge highlights this beauty by showing how Milton wove real events into the imaginative and colorful language of his poems without sounding a false note. It is necessary, therefore, to have some knowledge of historical forces which shaped Milton's England to understand and appreciate *Paradise Lost*.

As pointed out previously, Milton lived during the historical period of England generally known as the Puritan Revolution. This Revolution, however, was by no means a mere religious conflict. It extended to the whole question of who should have sovereignty—the king or the people.

On the one hand were the Monarch and the Episcopal Church, who believed in the Divine Right of Kings; on the other were the Parliamentarians, a group composed largely of Presbyterians, who believed in constitutional monarchy and the right of the people to delegate all earthly authority. However, it was a religious as well as a political struggle, in which the Presbyterians were, in fact, concerned with carrying on in England the aims of the Reformation begun in Germany by Martin Luther. They wished to eliminate the hierarchy and ritual of the Episcopal Church, and return to a simpler form of worship, with a democratic governing body. At its most ideal, the leaders of the Reformation sought a greater communication between the individual and God.

The idealistic Milton espoused both the political and religious causes, working, he thought, for "Christ's Kingdom" on earth. Later, he would also differ with the Presbyterians, returning to the vision of a more merciful God, as illustrated in *Paradise Lost*.

Beyond the religious and political struggle, Milton's age was full of lively controversy in the areas of science, morals and education. The scheme of the Universe was a subject for fiery debate, for the first telescopes turned the old world upside down, and the shape of the Universe was under dispute.

Paradise Lost was affected by all of these arguments and involved Milton's dearest beliefs. Perhaps the most colorful passages in the poem are paraphrases of his real life experiences. Versed in statesmanship, having heard the greatest oratory of the day in the parliamentary debates of that revolutionary time, the informal council of Book II of *Paradise Lost* is like a super-human parliamentary debate. Many critics have compared the fire and passion of Satan's speeches to the most famous oratory of Cromwell.

In the very beginning of the book, Milton invokes the Muse for his success, and spotted throughout the poem are Christian prayers. In Milton's later works this is not found; why then in *Paradise Lost*? Again and again Milton speaks of his blindness, of his consoling love for beauty, his inward vision compensating for the dark world outside.

Milton always allied himself with the democratic arguments of the Puritan Party, but his religious attitude underwent considerable change. Eventually, he found himself almost as much at odds with the conventional Presbyterians as with the Episcopal Church.

By the time Milton wrote *Paradise Lost* he was a true independent. He no longer believed in the Calvinistic doctrine of predestination. God, like man and all of nature, was subject to the natural law of reason, and a reasonable God was not the arbitrary Jehovah of Calvin, who limited space in heaven to a pre-ordained few. Milton's God, therefore, is merciful, and allows salvation to all true believers. This, in fact, becomes the avowed theme of the poem.

In *Paradise Lost*, the principle of moral freedom of choice is declared and restated. Through this freedom of choice, God's treatment of mankind is justified. Adam and Eve sin knowingly. Their sin is not predetermined, but is of free choice. When God passes judgment, he tells the angels that

Adam and Eve had the power to choose right, but instead they chose wrong. When Adam tells the angel of his "weakness against the charm of beauty's powerful glance," the angel commands Adam to be the master of his own passions.

Hanford, in the *Milton Handbook*, comments, "In *Paradise Lost*, the justification of the divine way lies in the representation of Adam as a free agent and in the revelation of the working as God's grace which allows him and his descendants the opportunity for a new exercise of moral choice and of consequent salvation even after the fall. Naturally, in the poem, Milton does not elaborate the theological argument, but goes out of his way again and again to insist on the fact of Adam's freedom."

Even the crucifixion of Christ is played down in *Paradise Lost*. The Son saves man from eternal damnation by self-sacrifice, but only by giving man another chance. Man must redeem himself. No one else can pay for his sins.

Milton was also subject to the contradictions of his times. Though intellectually a democrat and believing in everyone's free right to choose, Milton had a deep distrust of man's ability to choose right from wrong. He never had contact with the common man and, though in early writings he claims trust for "the plain people" to choose their own church ministers (and in *Areopagitica* he sings to the intelligence of the English people), in other writings he expresses grave doubts about their moral awareness. His own love of freedom could not allow him to exclude others from this essential state. In *Paradise Lost*, even Satan in his dreadful hell comments to the other fallen angels, "Here at least we will be free."

In this work, Milton also sets forth the traditional Christian doctrine of the Chain of Being, in which Man ranks below the angels and God, but above animals, in spirituality. In the Chain of Being, the human female also ranks below the male. Because of this concept, Milton has often been accused of being a woman-hater. In this idea, however, Milton was merely following the Christian tradition. Eve's sin, therefore, being committed by a lesser creature, is not as great as Adam's, who carried a greater responsibility for his actions. As Milton states in Book IV: "He for God only, she for God in him."

Milton's attitude toward women was, of course, partly colored by his own marital problems, and his puritanical upbringing. He disliked the chivalric idea which placed women on a pedestal. He believed that men and women should share their work and their pleasures. Marital love must be chaste and devoid of lust, for lust could only bring sorrow. In *Paradise Lost*, Eve expresses time and time again her emotional dependency on Adam. He never reciprocates with similar feeling. Milton believed that a man and his wife must accept the superiority of the male and of the dependency and weakness of woman.

Milton was a knowledgeable and scholarly man, in touch with the new scientific discoveries of his day. In 1610, Galileo had confirmed the

Copernician theory of the solar system. The earth was replaced by the sun as the center of our universe. Milton knew and admired Galileo, as these lines from Book I show:

"The Tuscan artist (who) views
At evening from the top of Fesole
Or in Valdarno to descry new lands
Rivers or mountains in her spotty globe."

And yet, he used the old Ptolomaic cosmography as the setting for *Paradise Lost*—his defenders maintain that Milton chose the old cosmography simply because it was better for his artistic purpose. But this made him many enemies. Today, when man has reached the moon, this may seem a ridiculous controversy. But, in Milton's day, those who cared about scientific advancement felt he had joined the conservatives who tried to hold back the pioneers of knowledge.

Milton's actual beliefs as regards science are hard to discern. The new discoveries of limitless space undoubtedly impressed him, and influenced the canvas of this epic poem. In his private school, Milton taught many of the new scientific ideas. There is no doubt, however, that his respect for science is coupled with a warning that it is not the only or even the best way to discover eternal truths. In science, too, lay the road of pride. In Book VIII, via the inquiry on celestrial motion, he actually conveys this idea, which has considerable significance for our own time. Milton warns his students to stay away from "God's secrets," since some things are not meant for mortal knowledge. Thus, the cosmological descriptions in *Paradise Lost* were probably based partially on scientific knowledge, partially on fancy. Yet, just as Milton's description of Eden is the product of his romantic readings, the technical descriptions of cannon firing in Book VI was accurately taken from military textbooks.

Much of the material for *Paradise Lost* came from the Bible, of course. The names and characters of the demons are drawn from there, and much of the content follows the story in Genesis and the Psalms. But you will also find a great many allusions to heathen gods and classical religious thought, as in the various stories of the fallen angels.

Since Milton was a classical scholar as well as an admirer of Shakespeare, the structure of his poem shows the influence of both Greek and Elizabethan drama. But, while Shakespeare's characters often talk the common idiom of the day, the language in *Paradise Lost* is mostly of more heroic proportions.

As with Shakespeare, through the centuries many voices have raised the cry of plagiarism. But evidence is heavy that Milton was in reality a scholar, influenced by many literary sources. He used ancient phrases, not as plagiaries, but to refresh them for the modern reader.

Milton had a strong influence on later poets. Wordsworth, for example, cherished Milton, and thought of himself as is poetic heir. In his long poem, *Prelude*, Wordsworth actually avows that he is following in Milton's footsteps, that he wants to create a great English epic. Wordsworth also composed a sonnet that indicates his high esteem for the great poet.

Milton fused his genius, literary knowledge, and strong convictions in *Paradise Lost*. The poem thus becomes a vehicle for understanding an important stage in history, and a great literary experience. A modern writer can gain from *Paradise Lost*, among other things, an exemplary view of the interwining of one's faith into a literary creation without detracting from its artistry.

CHARACTER ANALYSIS

SATAN

The major figure for many readers is Satan, partially because he is strongwilled, partially because he is introduced early in the poem, partially because his speeches are so rhetorical and dramatic, and partially because some of the ideas he is arguing are on the surface receptive. What the writings of those who advance Satan to heroic stature indicate, however, is that they are not reading Books I and II carefully to discern the picture of Satan being presented. He does not deteriorate as the poem progresses: he is a liar and self-deceiver from the beginning; he warps ideas and colors opinion by pejorative (but not honest) language; he shows intemperance, illogicality, wrath, and deceit. Milton does present his material with the focus appropriate for the substance and context, so that Satan and his cohorts, looked at in Hell, appear giant figures engaged in colossal action and idea. But once Hell and its occupants are seen against other worlds and other inhabitants, it is refocussed as smaller and certainly petty of action and idea. (For analogy—without infernal implications—we might compare the importance to us of say a school election when we are in school and the refocus which will come as we move out into the larger world.) However, Milton has not been deceitful in creating this impression, for the two similes (of the bees and the fairies) which end Book I should make clear the discrepancy between Satan's point of view and the relative view encompassing all elements in all worlds.

Satan has been called "hero" apparently for two reasons: he enunciates ideas in Book I which on the surface appeal to the oppressed against unjust authority (such as the revolutionary world of Shelley would hold dear), and he engages in a questing voyage and a struggle with an opposing force. These had been usual earmarks for heroes of classical and Renaissance epics. The first reason disappears as reason when we reread Book I with full knowledge of the whole poem, and certainly when we look at it from Milton's beliefs and from the realization that the assumed "unjust authority" is an ultimately benevolent God. (Of course, if God is unacceptable to a critic, Satan will probably remain "hero.") The second reason really presents a heroic figure rather than a hero, and the seeming opposing force of God is not opposing in the sense that the outcome is never in question. This is part of Satan's self-delusion. If we must have a hero, perhaps we need a different definition from the classical type, one rather placing Man as "hero" in terms of a morality play. Implied is Man's quest as Adam and Eve leave Eden and start to follow the course of history laid out in Books XI and XII, and the struggle with the opposing force of evil which Man's sense of good will constantly encounter.

Satan as rhetorical underdog will probably continue to elicit adherents, but more analytic reading of the full poem will nullify his appeal. Beyond this we must remember that we are reading a work of literature, regardless of the momentous ideas which it incorporates, and that we should therefore not confuse it with nonfictional philosophy, as important as Milton's beliefs are to the poem.

GOD

Primarily as a result, first, of the popular advancement of Satan as hero and, secondly, of the nonacceptance of Milton's theology, the God of *Paradise Lost* has in the twentieth century been criticized as harsh, vindictive, and unjust. This attitude develops because of the separation of the godhead between Father and Son as speaking characters, because of the position of the Father as a kind of observer of the action, all of which He has foreseen, because the fallen angels cannot ever change their position according to the Father's words in Book III, and because of the feeling that Adam and Eve could not avoid falling. God the Father, of necessity, has to enunciate the law under which the action takes place. Any individual in authority runs a like risk of antagonism, e.g., the school official who must warn against plagiarism and pass a harsh judgment when plagiarism has occurred. God lays down the rules of the game played in the arena of life. The Son—who the critics forget is also God—presents love and mercy, and this emphasizes contrastingly the Father's statement of rules and judgment when the rules are broken. The Son's judgment in Book X is acceptable to God's critics because Satan has been so degenerated in their eyes by this time and because Adam and Eve are shown mercy.

At the center of criticism is the lack of acceptance that although God foresees, He does not ordain. If God foresees the fall, then it will have to occur, goes the argument; the answer, of course, is that if the fall was not to occur, God would not foresee it. Why doesn't God do something to stop Satan from entering Eden and assaulting Eve? it is asked. The reason is that the game is one where the winner is he who has shown himself worthy of heaven. Interference from God would remove the doctrine of freedom of will. Since God created the game, the rules are what He wants to make them. The game and the rules do not of themselves indicate winner and loser. Further, the existence of Sin has implied to many that God created it, or at least allowed it to come into being. And if He did, then He has "loaded the dice" against both Satan and Man. But Sin does not have substance, and is thus not "of God"; it is only essence. It does not exist for Eve until she falls, though some have argued otherwise. Once the convenant theology which underlies the epic is accepted, God does not appear as a culprit. *The reader's view of God does not really depend on Milton's presentation of Him, but on the reader's beliefs and understandings of what is happening in the poem.* We do not have so much a "character" presented in God as philosophic matter.

ADAM

The crux for the interpretation of Adam's character is his succumbing to the allurement of Eve. Adam falls because of uxoriousness, his love for Eve and her beauty, and his rejection of right reason and thus obedience in favor of her appeal to him. This fall in Book IX has been prepared for in Book VIII, as we have seen. Aside from this concern, the character of Adam has not elicited argument, probably because he tends to meld into the texture of the poem and does not stand out from it. His moral realizations in the last two books somewhat tend to characterize him as naive and impressionable, but more of their effect is philosophic than dramatic.

EVE

The character of Eve is created largely in Book IX, although we have been prepared for what happens there in Books IV and V. What we discern is a narcissistic personality, weak-willed and easily pliable of mind, one who thinks in terms of herself and her own needs. The effects of the fall, the despair of Book X with its possible suicide, and the discussions leading to hope because of the prophecy concerning Eve's progeny are significant in themselves rather than for the development of an attitude toward her. Eve, all investigators have concluded, presents a better opinion of women than was usual in seventeenth-century Puritanism. She is not presented as a mere possession of man, to do his bidding without question; she is not merely childbearer and housekeeper. Eve is not interested in such mental excursions as the cosmology of Book VIII (she would rather hear any of this from Adam) and she sleeps through the visions of the future. But though mentally inferior to Adam and though concerned with love for Adam, rather than for God, she is nonetheless presented as an individual who has feelings and personality, wrongly disposed though they may be.

STYLE

Critics and fellow poets have praised Milton's poetic skill even when they have reacted adversely to his theology or to his personality or to specific parts of *Paradise Lost*. For example, J. H. B. Masterman in his history of seventeenth-century literature sees many weaknesses in the epic, but then he calls Milton's poetry "the utmost measure of attainable excellence in metrical form." It is difficult to define wherein the greatness of poetry (as of music) lies, but some simple facts about Milton's prosody should be noted.

Paradise Lost is written in blank verse, that is, unrhymed iambic pentameter. (In other words, the lines have five feet, each foot usually consisting of two syllables, with the accent on the second syllable.) In order to have the sound reflect the sense, or for variety and effectiveness, Milton frequently substitutes spondees (feet of two accented syllables) and trochees (feet of two syllables, with the first syllable stressed, the following unstressed) for the more regularly employed iambs. The use of blank verse, unbroken by set stanzas, permits the author to develop his ideas briefly or at length, unhampered by a predetermined pattern.

Milton as a well-educated man of the seventeenth century wrote in Latin with almost as much ease as in English. It is not surprising, then, that his choice of words (his diction) seems to our modern ears to be highly Latinized. One interesting point rises here. As Professor Frank Patterson, Milton's great modern editor, used to tell his classes, Milton presumably expected his reader to have in mind the original Latin word as well as the later English word derived from it. Accordingly he hoped that through these connotations words with a Latin source would have added values or bring more vivid pictures to mind. For example, in Book I, line 46, when Satan was hurled from Heaven with "hideous ruin," the Latin word *ruina,* meaning "a falling down," adds to the picture value. Or, when in Book VI, line 619, Satan mockingly speaks of the use of gunpowder against the angels as having a "quick result"; the Latin source of the word *result* gives a picture of the victims "leaping back." One other influence of Milton's Latin scholarship should be noted: his frequent inversions in word order; these do not surprise the ear of anyone accustomed to Latin sentence structure.

To emphasize his points and to appeal to the aesthetic senses of his readers, Milton uses many references, metaphors, and similes. (See the comment on Book I for a discussion of his Homeric similes.) For his comparisons he usually drew upon the Bible and upon classical mythology and literature. He lived in a period when a man of any education was far better acquainted with the Bible and the classics than most people are today. But even in his own day Milton was exceptionally well-read—remember that he devoted his life to study until after he was thirty. (It is obviously unfair to accuse him of making a deliberate display of his learning.)

From time to time Milton has passages with many proper names, usually of gods or places. One excellent critic, J. A. Symonds, said that these lists are "magnificent for their mere gorgeousness of sound." Later critics have pointed out that these lists serve a more specific purpose at various points. C. S. Lewis, for instance, claims the sound of these "splendid, remote, terrible, voluptuous, or celebrated things" suggests the richness and variety of the world, and so gives us a needed background for the action.

A minor device that Milton again and again uses effectively is to add a second adjective (or qualifying phrase) to an already modified noun. He speaks of "heavy days and cruel," the "upright heart and pure," "a sad task and hard." Here Milton is showing—and making good use of—another side of his culture. T. H. Prince, a modern critic, has shown this was common usage in the Italian poetry of Dante and Petrarch, two of the English poet's favorite authors.

In noting these obvious points about Milton's prosody, the reader should not forget Milton's prevailing genius, what one of his earlier editors (James Prendeville) called one of the rarest perfections of poetry: the perfect "assimilation of the sound and the sense."

REVIEW QUESTIONS

1. How much of *Paradise Lost* is Biblical? How much is classical?

2. Discuss Milton's use of parallelism in *Paradise Lost*.

3. Trace and explain the average reader's changing emotional reaction to Milton's Satan.

4. Discuss briefly Addison's theory that in *Paradise Lost* Milton has two Eves, two Adams.

5. Eve is considered to be the most complicated character in *Paradise Lost*, and her motivation in her acts never seems to be simple and direct. Try to show the various sides of Eve as they are revealed both before and after the Fall.

6. Discuss Adam as the logical hero of *Paradise Lost*.

7. What is your intellectual and emotional reaction to *Paradise Lost*?

8. Milton twice uses the leviathan image, Book I, lines 201-209, and Book VII, lines 412-416. Briefly discuss these two similes.

9. In Book I is there any significance in the way Satan and Beelzebub refer to God?

NOTES

NOTES